# The

# DARK SIDE OF STARTUPS

Arvind Arora ◊ Pranesh Jain

*Published by :*

**Invincible Publication Pvt.Ltd.**

***Published by:***

***Invincible Publication Pvt. Ltd.***

***201A, SAS Tower, Sector 38, Gurugram, Haryana – 122003***
***Phone: +91-124-4034247, +91 9599066061***
***Website : www.invinciblepublishers.com***

***Sales Office : - 4760-61/23, Basement, Pratap Street, Ansari Road,***
***Daryaganj, New Delhi - 110002***
***Phone: +91-11-40198405***
***Email: invinciblepublishers@gmail.com***



***ISBN : 978-81-963918-2-9***

***Book Name : Dark Side of Startups***


***First Edition: August 2023***

Special Thanks

To

*Sagar Setia*

&

Revika Malik, Raveena Paul, Shashi Prakash Diwedi,
Jagriti Arvind Arora, CA Deepti Pranesh Jain,
CS Nikita Sharma, CA Vipin Patidar,
CS Shraddha Diya, Arpit Pareek, CA Kashish Kathuria,
Mudit Thakkar, Sanjay Kumar

# Contents

## Part -1

## Part -2

# PREFACE

ARVIND ARORA

On the morning of March 4, 2023, at 10 o'clock, my wife's mobile began to receive social media notifications. The comment box was flooded with remarks like "Arvind Arora is a fraud", "Arvind Arora is a cheater", and similar comments. Not only about me, but people also left derogatory comments on my wife's social media posts. Seeing these comments, my wife started feeling anxious, her breathing quickened, and suddenly, she sat down on the couch, visibly shaken. Witnessing her distress, my anxiety doubled as she wasn't feeling well. To be honest, the fear wasn't about whether what was happening was right or wrong, but the concern was the impact it would have on my wife, who was nurturing the hope within her belly. This was the child for whom both of us, as husband and wife, had waited for 12 years. We had been nurturing the dream of cradling this child in our arms for years. Perhaps, this dream was finally going to come true, but before it could, everything ended abruptly.

The stream of negative comments was ongoing when some investors who had invested in my startup started calling, asking for their invested amounts. Several investors began issuing threats of fraud and taking legal action. What hurt the most was that my social media friends stopped supporting me, began avoiding my calls, and eventually, everyone distanced themselves from me. It felt as if within a single day, a negative perception of Arvind Arora had taken root in people's minds.

My wife's stress level was increasing; she had never seen so much negativity in her life before. I wasn't sure how would I manage to handle her? I deleted all the social media apps from her phone, but I couldn't erase anything from her mind. This incident occurred around 7 PM on March 4, 2023. I was trying my best to overcome all these difficulties.... suddenly, my wife fainted and fell While going to the bathroom. Until she regained consciousness, our lives were waiting for news that perhaps neither of us ever wanted to hear. That day, we lost the hope we had been considering as our child.

Unfortunately, our dream of becoming parents remained incomplete............

My one mistake of starting a startup had turned our lives into hell. That day, it felt like whether I really had the right to ruin so many lives together. All of you must be wondering what happened that day that I am saying this.

Actually, last night, the episode of Shark

Tank Season 2 for my startup was released. Due to fantastic pitching and confidence, I made it through two rounds and reached the finals. However, in the third round, I couldn't hold on for too long against the sharks. This resulted in us not getting funding. The most significant thing at that time was that I was on national television. Despite being a teacher or a YouTube influencer, I was in front of the sharks on the biggest stage of a startup. For me, starting a startup or understanding business was not an easy task. After the episode, my wife said that the show went well and I was unnecessarily worried. It was true that I wasn't feeling positive vibes for the episode of Shark Tank, and because of this, I had even requested not to AIR the episode of Shark Tank India. I will tell you why I wanted to do that, but it's not the right time now. That night, my mom also called. She was very happy and said, "My son has come on TV." Because of this, I was extremely happy.

Now, I was also feeling that my Shark Tank episode went well, although it was disappointing that funding didn't happen. No funding was obtained. Although, the sharks pulled my leg, but I didn't have any objection to it because I didn't have much experience in startups and business by that time. For me, appearing on Shark Tank was merely a platform for learning, nothing more than that. We felt that even if we didn't get funding, at least the name of the startup would be known to everyone, and for those who invested, worked, or supported in the company, it would be a matter of great pride. We were also very happy about this aspect.

After the episode, around 11:30 PM at night, a call came in... This call was from that teacher who was shown in the shark tank demo in the app demonstration at the Shark Tank telecast upon the recommendation of the sharks out of our 65 course teachers. I thought it might be a "thank you" call for "choosing me out of 60+ courses" because appearing on national TV is a big deal. But what she said  was mind-boggling... she said, "I feel insulted because your company didn't get funding. Now either remove my video from that episode immediately, or compensate me." Now, all the rights to the video are with the television and she knew that I was incapable of doing all this because I have no control over the channel's content rights, nor does anyone else, and in this way, we understood that she indirectly wanted money from us. She also hinted at tarnishing my and the company's image on social media, If we didn't provide her the compensation what she was demanding from me.

You know how sometimes things go beyond our imagination? Well, this was one of those instances. That teacher collaborated with some former individuals associated with the company, including the ex-co-founder, ex-employees, and consultants, to use social media as a weapon to damage my reputation and bring negative attention to the company. They all joined forces and posted a viral message on social media under the name "We need support," all with the intent to tarnish my image and push for action against the company.

Tagging my name with various individuals, they orchestrated the content to go viral, and everyone collectively engaged in disrespectful comments and false accusations to tarnish my image. Many people reacted without knowing the truth, which deeply saddened me, those who were supported me and helped me to become a YouTube influencer were now without knowing proper information, contributing to those negative responses.

Even up to this point, I was enduring everything, including the fact that some YouTube channels had edited my Shark Tank clips to mock me and attempted to portray it as if the sharks had insulted me greatly during the episode. The posts went viral all over the internet. I received a lot of backlash in the comment section. My name was subjected to a lot of false accusations. Now, I am concerning about my career also, I began to worry as issues were emerging from all sides.

With all these problems, the former founders and consultants of the company showcased these incidents to investors, stirring them up, to demand their investment back from the company. Investors started calling me, not to congratulate or offer support during tough times, but to demand their money back. At that time, I kept my composure and gathered all the evidence for the future, whether it was the viral posts, inappropriate comments, or investor threats.

Up until a day before the Shark Tank episode, everything was fine, but within a few hours, my life completely changed. Friends who used to answer my calls immediately were now unreachable, and when I needed their support on social media, they didn't even pick up my calls. No one came forward to support me. After one attack followed another, my wife and I lost our child due to the stress. We stayed indoors for five days due to depression, and for several days, we didn't even open our social media accounts. I kept my phone off, hoping that at least my problem, created deliberately by others, wouldn't affect me and my wife, now my focus was just on staying safe and calm. At that time, various questions were swirling in my mind. I was wondering why I had entered Shark Tank in the first place. What made me to take such a big risk?

I'm sharing this for the first time that we

haven't had a child for the past 12 years, and it was the first time we were fortunate enough to be parents of a child. The importance of this can be understood by everyone. Certainly, now I have nothing to loose. Even though I feel that after losing so much, there might not be anything left to loose, but as life never stops for anyone; it just keeps moving forward. So, I gathered myself again after all that loss. I explained to my wife and showed her the courage to rise once more, so that we could step out of that dark world and move towards the light.

Coming on Shark Tank 2 was the biggest mistake of my life. After that, so many unexpected things happened in my Persnal life. In life, many times we can only see what our eyes want to see or, in other words, what is shown to us but in reality, there are many events behind the scenes that can be very painful. After the Shark Tank episode, many videos were viralized to boost channel TRP ratings. Some YouTube channels also viral the videos to increase their subscribers, and a content creator did a lot of things incorrectly just to earn money and fame. Many people have seen all of this and given their reactions.

By that time, I had realized that nowadays, people seem to value personal fame and money more than humanity and compassion. During those five days, I realized that countless founders like me might have turned their lives into a hell to transform their startups into unicorns. The façade of a unicorn might appear gloriously pure, but the nights spent creating it is often equally dark. How much burden of investors' money does a founder bear? In this country, there are countless startup founders who, like me, have experienced life's challenges. The more I learn about the lives of founders in the startup world, the more my curiosity grows.

That's when I met my co-author, Pranesh Jain. He had several years of experience to handle various startups. Being a Chartered Accountant by profession, he provided me with the opportunity to understand the mindset of startup founders, investors, advisors, and people working in startups. During our discussions, I learned that there are many startup founders in the country who have sacrificed a lot to make their startups successful. Some founders ended their careers; while others saw their families fall apart. Some got entangled in legal disputes, while others were consumed by addictions and depression.

However, all these startup founders are now lost in the dark world of startups. Currently, startups are the talk of the town in the country, and there is zeal among the youth to start their own ventures, which I don't consider wrong. But I believe that if the youth enter the field of startups with a better understanding, victory is certain. Me and my co-author Pranesh Jain, just want these entrepreneurial minds to take calculated risks and not jump in without knowing the entire picture. With this goal in mind, this book has been written, titled "The darkside of Startups," because the path to light emerges from darkness. Understanding the dark side of startups will eventually lead you and your startup to success one day.

PRANESH JAIN

On the full night of April 6, 2023, I spent the entire time sitting at the system, understanding all the issues related to a fledgling startup. On one hand, the startup founders were preparing to bring in new investments to rescue the company from closure, and on the other hand, I was gearing up for the due diligence process scheduled for the company. Because I knew that if the company's due diligence report turned out to be adverse, the investment could be halted. It is very challenging for us as similar to what a doctor might experience in the ICU while treating a patient in serious condition.

The founders were working day and night to save the company and benefit the investors. Amidst all this, my role as the company's consultant was to fix their troubled accounting system and provide them with all the documents required by the investors for due diligence. It was a strange situation; the founders were running the company while also managing the pressure from the investors. I hadn't witnessed such a scenario before. In my years of experience, I dealt with many clients who kome to me in similar situations, struggling with these kinds of complexities.

I take pride in the fact that I have helped numerous people during my tenure, when a chartered accountant sits at the system, attempting to understand the various issues that can impact a funded startup, it becomes necessary to ponder how valuable a time the chartered accountant is dedicating to shaping the future of that startup. It is also crucial to recognize the gravity and significance of the subject. Now, you might be wondering how I, being a chartered accountant, would know what is essential for a startup. Here, I would like to say that my expertise lies in forensic audits and startup funding. Since I am well-versed in these matters, it's evident that my clients are happy and satisfied with my consultancy. I charge them a good fee for this, which may not compensate my family time, but it does cover my wife's expenses for sure. Hahaha! Jokes a Part!!! Moving Ahead......

Coming back to the issue at hand... while

working through that entire night, a thought kept circling in my mind: why is such a situation arising in startups? Are startups genuinely succeeding, or is it just a façade of success being presented?

As this thought was running through my mind, at the same time, my friend Arvind Arora, who was in Bangalore, was also pondering over the same matter. When he called me, we discussed these issues at length. It was this very conversation that inspired us to prepare this content. In the past years, I have personally witnessed the making and the breaking of a lot of startups. I've witnessed some startups succeed and some fail despite their efforts. Nowadays, everywhere you look, people are talking about unicorn startups. However, amidst all this, many startups have disappeared, and nobody knows about them. I believe that in today's scenario, it's essential for young individuals to understand the other side of startups, which might provide them with a more accurate perspective before diving into the startup world. In this book, we have made an effort to explain the technical aspects of startups in a simple and conversational language, rather than using technical jargon, to help you better understand the startup world.

In this book, we have integrated all those facets of startups that perhaps no founder, consultant, or employee would even want to discuss. While creating this book, we also engaged in discussions with several founders, which aided us in presenting all the dimensions of startups in a better way. When you are striving to create something different in your life (a startup), everything seems right, because at that moment, you can only see its positive aspects. However, this is where mistakes often begin, as you're only focusing on the positive side.

# Unit-1

# DARK
# SIDE OF
# STARTUPS

Everyone has witnessed the glamour of Bollywood in the film industry. Similarly, the glamour of startups has also become a topic of discussion in the business world. Today, in our country, the founders of all unicorn startups have also become celebrities. Just as behind the glamour of Bollywood, there are many hidden truths, the world of startups also holds some dark realities beneath its glamour.

No person can ever completely stop dreaming, and dreaming isn't a bad thing either. Today, in our country, many young individuals are aspiring to start startups and turn them into unicorns. Some have already transformed their dreams into reality, while others are very close to making their dreams come true. There's no age limit for starting a startup. You might have seen old age startup founders on popular TV shows like Shark Tank India, whose passion for startups shines through regardless of their age.

Today, many startups in the country have shut down. Some have reached the brink of closure due to a lack of further funding, including several unicorn startups. Many startup founders have wasted their careers and time, returning to working jobs in other companies. Several startup founders are struggling with depression and high levels of stress. In the startup culture of the country, founders and employees are working tirelessly, and a significant portion of them have fallen into the traps of addiction and smoking.

Over the past few years, numerous startups have closed down, where founders not only invested their own funds but also roped in their family's savings and investments alongside the investor funds. There are several startups in the country that are incurring significant losses and are resorting to ethical, unethical, legal, or even illegal means to secure future funding. Because if further funding isn't obtained, the inevitable fate of the startup is its closure.

"This is the reason why many startups in the country have posed new challenges in recent years. These startups, in their haste, employ multiple employees simultaneously in the company. Similarly, due to the lack of funding, many employees are also being laid off without a notice period. Startups spend an immense amount of money on marketing and branding after receiving funding. Many unicorn startups are still wasting money on sponsorship and personal branding at big events. Over the past few years, startups have received substantial support and funding from investors, allowing startup founders to spend money according to their own will. Most cash burn is mainly focused on two areas:

first, keeping more employees on the job than required, and second, excessive spending on marketing and branding."

"Because startups aren't going to receive funding in the future, the end of the startup is inevitable."

"Most of the cash burn is used to increase the company's valuation. In the pursuit of increasing valuation, most startups and startup founders headed on to the wrong path, where the startup's valuation may increase, but its profitability and sustainability are completely eroded. Many startups still inflate their valuation by showcasing fake sales, while some startups spend more on acquiring customers through sales than the money they receive from sales."

"In recent times, funding in startups has been decreasing, which is causing fewer visible improvements in the startup ecosystem. Continuous layoffs are also being observed in startups. The valuation of startups for investment is becoming a critical factor, and startups are finding it challenging to attract investors.

A significant change can be observed in the startup landscape, where investors are now focusing not only on valuation but also on the profitability and sustainability of startups. This shift indicates a more mature and cautious approach from investors. They are looking for startups that not only have the potential for rapid growth but also have a clear plan to generate consistent revenue and become sustainable in the long run. This change in investor mindset encourages startups to develop more robust business models, streamline operations, and prioritize achieving profitability with growth. It ultimately contributes to a healthier and more sustainable startup ecosystem.

Recently, a major VC firm conducted a special audit for startup founders and their transactions because investors believe that some startup founders have misused investor funding. Such actions have been observed in several startups. On the contrary, some startup founders have faced actions taken against them by their smaller investors due to disagreements. While some founders are doing excellent work in their startups, they often struggle to scale up the company according to their vision due to investor interference.

In today's country, there are many young individuals who start their own startups by leaving their education in between. Several of these youth have even chosen to start a startup instead of pursuing degrees from prestigious institutions like IITs and IIMs. This can be a risky endeavor. Nowadays, many young people are influenced by the stories of unicorn startup founders and prominent personalities, leading them to start startups as a form of showmanship. In the world of startups, genuine problem-solving startups are rare to find, but those focused on appearances and founders who portray themselves as entrepreneurs can be seen everywhere.

Even today, only around 10% of startups are truly capable of addressing real problems, while the remaining 90% get influenced by the glamour showcased in programs like Shark Tank and the success stories of unicorn founders, leading them to start businesses. Many young individuals, driven by the luxurious lives of unicorn founders in the country, have wasted their time chasing the startup dream. Some youngsters have been inspired by the success stories of college-going startup founders and have started their own ventures based on such influences.

If you want to be successful, it's essential for you to understand the ground reality of a startup.

As much attention as startups are drawing from the youth in the country, there are equally as many challenges being observed within the startup landscape. "The Dark Side of Startups" is a book prepared to illuminate the issues behind startups and to provide the younger generation with an understanding of startups. The aim is to prevent them from making mistakes and to guide them in the right direction to successfully build their startups with careful thought and consideration.

> The Success of the young entrepreneur will be the Key to India's Transformation in the new Millennium.
>
> **- Dhirubhai Ambani**

# Cautiousness in the allotment of company Shares in the initial days of the Startup

# 1

Whenever a company begins, numerous individuals extend their interest in joining it and also express their interest in holding shares in the company's ownership. A startup founder, in the initial days, doesn't contemplate how much their business's value will increase in the future or what might happen. They only desire, to have good people associated with them, and due to this reason, this decision doesn't appear too tough for them. The mistake here is that the only thing that goes wrong is the ownership of shares that they want to give. Are they providing it with any written commitment? And if not, when that individual intends to exit from the company, what situation will emerge at that time? How will they deal with it? This is a thought-provoking issue. It is crucial for a founder to understand that in the early days of a startup, ownership should solely remain with the founder and co-founders. If you are considering making someone a co-founder who is a close friend or an associate, it's important to have a proper agreement in writing with them as well.

Not too long ago, We encountered a peculiar situation in a funded startup. A founder had given 2% equity shares to a colleague based on informal commitments. This colleague was supposed to work together and contribute to the company's growth. However, within just two months, he had to go abroad for further studies. In this situation, based on verbal commitments, the allocated 2% equity shares ended up with someone who hadn't contributed anything to the company. Now, when the company's valuation reached 7.5 crores, the value of that person's shares had risen to 15 lakhs. It's astonishing how a single mistake could have such significant consequences for a company. Although founders and the company have legal options with them, but here the question is whether they have enough time and money for such an exhausting process. Give it a thought...

# Raising funds without proper understanding and conducting a funding round at an incorrect valuation

# 2

When a startup decides to raise funds, it's essential to have a clear understanding of its financials, market potential, growth projections, and the value it brings to investors. Choosing the right valuation is crucial because it determines how much ownership you have to give away in exchange for the funds.

These days, the trend of startup funding has become quite popular. Even on national television, shows about startup investments are highly prevalent. Startups are emerging in every corner of the country, and investors are putting money into startups even from small towns of the country. This indicates that awareness about investment in startups is increasing. However, along with this, problems are also increasing.

We believe that it's very important for new startup founders to be aware of these issues.

Many times We think about how startup founders make decisions about their company's valuation on their own terms. You might be wondering how this is possible, but this is India, my friend. Here, everything is possible, and you might feel like it's all a bit chaotic. To understand how this happens, let's explore the methods of calculating startup valuation. The valuation of any startup company is determined by registered valuers or merchant bankers based on its future cash flows. Here, a startup founder can showcase the company's envisioned future, and the valuation can be presented accordingly. This makes it easier for smaller startups to raise funding. However, they might not realize that today's solution could become a significant problem for them tomorrow, and they are unaware of the challenges that might arise in the future. Currently, you will observe that even at the pre-revenue stage, meaning the early stages of business startups, young entrepreneurs are raising funding at valuations ranging from 10 to 20 crores. Now, you might ask, what's wrong if investors are putting money into startups at those valuations? We've previously discussed that in smaller startups, money is being invested by individuals who might not have a true investor mindset. Usually, due to the advice of certain advisors or personal connections, these individuals are investing in startups, and this isn't necessarily a bad thing.

Here, our point is directed towards startup founders. After raising funds at incorrect valuations, where could problems arise for you in the future?

Now, we need to understand this situation through an example. Let's consider a startup founder who establishes a company and just 20 days after its inception, manages to secure funding of 20 lakhs at a valuation of 10 crores. This funding is meant to help them develop their product. After about 2 months, the product is ready, and the development cost totals 15 lakhs. They started selling the product. They spend a lot of amount on marketing and on forming a new team. Now if the sales are good and everything is in favor, he might achieve the forecasted valuation in some time. But if the sale doesn't go well, the founder will have a tough time in raising funds at such a high valuation. In this case, either he will have to decrease the valuation, which might not be accepted by the previous investors or they can inject their own personal savings into the business. The latter option, in our opinion, could be a risky decision, as it might deplete all personal savings and might not yield the desired results.

In the end, even if they consider getting an unsecured loan from a bank, it might not be a suitable solution in this scenario.

This situation teaches us that it's crucial not to get carried away by appearances and to raise funds from investors at the right valuation for your startup. It might even require giving up slightly more equity if needed, but starting with an incorrect valuation can lead you in trouble in the near future. Founders often realize this when they raise funds at a high valuation and then end up burning through the capital, only to understand the reality much later.

It's essential for founders to understand that the short-term satisfaction of raising funds at a high valuation can lead to long-term challenges. Making the decision to raise funds at a valuation that accurately reflects the startup's potential and stage can save you from future hardships.

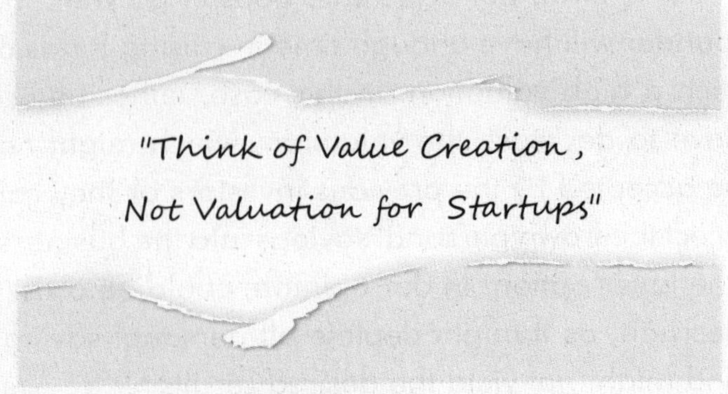

# Leaving A Profitable Business To Begin With A Startup

# 3

Sometimes We feel that in our country, there are many young individuals who come from capable families, and their families are engaged in highly profitable businesses. However, nowadays, it seems like every other youth in the country wants to start a startup. When they go to college, they are also taught and encouraged about startup-related matters. In such a situation, any young person wouldn't prefer to continue the family business using the old methods, because they don't get the same level of independence there that they could achieve through their own startup. Hence, they work hard with a passion for starting their own startup, leaving behind the family's profitable business. Although there is nothing wrong with this, we believe that we have seen many successful startups where young individuals have carved out a new identity for their family's profitable business in the world of startups. It's crucial that if you are starting a startup, you focus on making it sustainable first, and then make it profitable. In the rush to scale a startup, don't forget both the factors of sustainability and profitability.

"It is very important that if you are starting a startup, you should first focus on making it sustainable, and then make it profitable. In the rush to scale a startup, don't forget both the factors of sustainability and profitability."

In conclusion, we would like to say that a startup doesn't become successful just by becoming a unicorn; but it truly succeeds when it becomes sustainable and profitable on its own. From where your... startup can naturally scale understand from that day all your decisions will be right, whether they involve investment funding or bank loans.

A BUSINESS WITHOUT A PATH TO PROFIT ISN'T A BUSINESS, IT'S ONLY HOBBY.

**- Jason Fried**

# Choosing to start a Startup instead of working a job

# 4

Whenever we hear the word "job," we envision a large segment of society that sustains their entire family solely through these jobs. Even today, there are many young individuals who are working in a company job but are also constantly seeking opportunities to start a startup. Some get the chance and leave their jobs to pursue a startup. Some individuals even start their startups while still holding a job, until they gain enough confidence that their startup is doing well.

There are approximately many such startups in the country, whose founders initially worked in jobs and then started their own startups. However, most of the startups that have shut down have led their founders to return to jobs. There are also founders who have started new startups again, and they are still striving to make themselves and their startups better in the startup world.

In our opinion, both options are not bad. If you are currently working in job and want to switch to starting a startup for something new, then undoubtedly, all paths in the startup world are open for you. Conversely, if you have become frustrated with the startup life and are worried about the success of your startup, you can always return to a job.

Now the issue is how to understand whether to stay in a job, switch to a startup, or transition from startups to a job? You will need to assess whether your current work is allowing you to maintain your survival. Make this decision for yourself and work accordingly. If you know that your survival is at risk and yet you continue to pursue the hope of your startup's success, then in my opinion, you might be putting yourself and your family through hardship. Although some fortunate startup founders have faced such situations and are now at the pinnacle of success. This is a very difficult decision for anyone to make. You can go from zero to a hundred, and you can also go from a hundred back to zero.

# Leaving a job relying on government schemes of Startups

## 5

These days, our government is introducing quite beneficial schemes to promote startups. The benefit of these schemes is being reaped by those budding startups that had a small idea but needed some support to enter the market. There are several government schemes that provide assistance in funding for many startups. However, it's not necessary that your startup will become successful solely through the funds provided by the government. The government only offers a small amount of funding to startups as a form of support, which helps you advance your company. But sometimes, it also happens that due to delays in receiving these funds, your startup could face difficulties and challenges.

There are also startup founders who, alongside their jobs, start their own startups and secure government funding proposals for their startups during the initial phase. Driven by this enthusiasm, they leave their steady jobs and fully focus on their startups. In such situations, you gain a lot of experience and learning that can be immensely beneficial for your startup's growth.

It's essential to make thoughtful decisions. If you don't receive government funding on time or the funds the company have with it, run out, how will you manage future funding for your startup? This is a crucial aspect to consider. Before availing funds from any government scheme and before leaving your steady job, it's important to contemplate how your decisions will affect your or your family's survival.

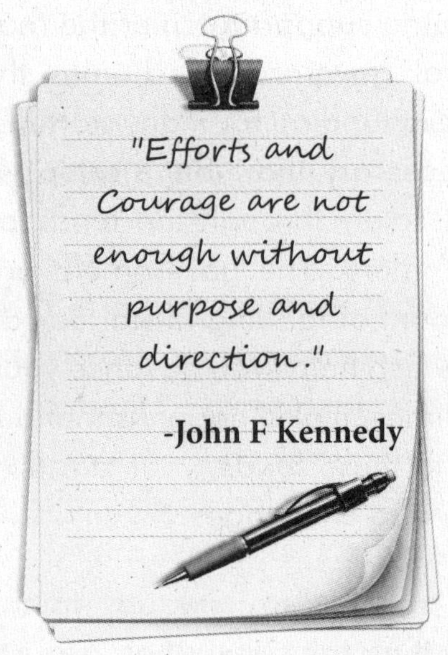

# Turning investors into founders in a Startup

# 6

Often, when we write a book, ther are certain subjects within it that feels the best and most engaging to us. Similarly, we felt the same while writing this book – there was a particular subject that resonated strongly with us. We thoroughly enjoyed writing about this subject, and that's why we'd like to show a slight bias here and say that this is the most intriguing story in the book.

Writing about this is quite challenging for us, as it isn't about the dark side of startups; instead, it's about the intricate web spun to erase the existence of the founder. It's like a maze that many startup founders have become trapped in. We have even seen episodes like this in a popular program on national television, where startup founders have given the investor a major stake in their company, essentially making them a founder and giving them the authority to make all decisions within the company.

Let's understand this from a very close perspective. Startups are considered an achievement for any founder. To put it simply, a startup is a founder's story of struggle, which doesn't make them an employee, but rather an owner. In any startup, the rights of investors are quite limited. While investors do gain ownership rights in startups, they don't have any direct involvement in the company's business operations. This means that founders in startups have complete freedom to run the business and make decisions independently.

We believe you've understood our point now. If you turn your investor into a founder, it could potentially limit your freedom to make decisions. It's also possible that the original purpose for which you started the startup might get lost, and you end up becoming an employee in your own company. This idea is also echoed in a Hindi film song that goes, "Naa bap bada na bhaiya, sabse bada rupaiya" (Money is the biggest of them all). When you're using the investor's money and they become your co-founder, your dependency on the investor could extend to every decision within the company. Sometimes, investors might even have their own businesses in the same segment, allowing them to dominate the startup and founder to eliminate competition. This can be referred to as corporate politics as well.

With such wrong steps, you could find yourself trapped in a web where you might have to deal with troubles, and it's possible that you could even be pushed out of your startup. A few years ago, two founders from Mumbai IIT started an innovative healthcare device company. They worked diligently to create an innovative product combining technology and healthcare. They secured funds from a handful of angel investors to develop this device. After the product was ready, the company needed funding to manufacture and market the product. To fulfill this need, they closed their next funding round with an individual who was given equity in the company and became a co-founder. The investor was financially capable, spent six months understanding the product, and grasped its market potential.

Afterwards, the investor brought individuals from his team into the company, who assisted the founders in product manufacturing and understood the intricacies of the product along with the founders. Over the course of a year, the investor gained a strong grip on the product, business, and market. Subsequently, the investor began to create difficulties within the company and started pressuring the founders. Gradually, the investor took complete control of the company and put pressure on the founders to the extent that they had no choice but to resign from the company for their own survival. At that time, the founders weren't even given money according to the company's valuation, and due to their circumstances, they were forced to leave the company.

Startup founders must understand that there are two crucial factors in every startup. First, managing the company according to their vision and second, bringing in investor funding for the company's future success. When you bring an investor as a founder of the company, even small decisions of the company become dependent on the investor's approval. Many times, we have seen that even for securing investor funding, founders have to rely solely on that particular investor because, for personal reasons, the investor doesn't allow the founder to approach any other investor for investment. This puts founders in a very serious situation.

Although some startups have succeeded after making an investor a founder and working hard to make them successful, these situations are far from ideal and can be very challenging for founders.

# In hopes of securing funding from the Startup, one invested all of his/her personal savings

## 7

It might seem unusual to hear that a founder can invest their entire savings into a startup with the hope that one day the startup will succeed and all the invested money will be returned as profits. However, this situation is quite common in the world, not just in our country. Many founders find themselves in such a position where they put all their savings on the line, even if they don't want to.

When you start your own startup, initially, you often run the company using your own funds and prepare the product at the pre-revenue stage. Sometimes, funding is obtained at this pre-revenue stage, but this is quite rare. In most cases, you have to start your startup using your personal savings or family savings.

When you begin to receive funding and advance your company, you become involved in the game of valuation and funding rounds. Since investors remain invested in the company and founders also draw their remuneration from there, which they set aside as savings for their future, as the company grows, their remuneration also increases.

As the company expands, their remuneration grows proportionally. When the company needs new funding but the subsequent rounds can't be closed for some reason, the company experiences a cash burn, and founders find themselves in a situation where future prospects are uncertain due to the lack of new funding.

In the absence of new funding, founders have a few options for the future. One option is to sell the company and exit, although this isn't always straightforward, especially when investors have invested in the company. The second option might be to shut down the company, which also isn't easy because of the invested funds from investors.

When the situation reaches a point where selling the company isn't feasible and closing it down isn't an easy decision either, there are usually two main choices. Either sell the company and take exit which not easy being a founder as investors fund is invested in the company or second choice is company can keep running for a few more months by arranging some funds and preparing for a new funding round. The hope is that things will improve after securing new funding. In this scenario, founders often reinvest the savings they had taken as remuneration back into the company.

This decision often involves emotional factors for founders. However, in the market, it's important to not appear or portray about the company that it is going through a dire phase, as that might raise questions about how viable it is for future investments. Many venture capital funds in the market invest smaller amounts in these companies, often for a fee of around 4-5% of the investment, understanding that sustaining a company can be extremely challenging.

Founders indeed don't want to extinguish their last bit of hope. That's why they often invest their savings into keeping the company operational until funding comes in. This allows the company to continue running smoothly without encountering major issues until a funding round is successfully raised. It's worth mentioning for your information that in companies, founders often convert the loans they provided to the company into equity before investors inject their funds. Founders can't usually repay their personal loans from the investors' funds that they originally invested just to rescue the company.

## "THE DARKSIDE OF STARTUPS"

## YOUR THOUGHTS ON DARK SIDES OF STARTUPS

Name :

Contact Number :

CHAPTER REVIEW NOTE -1

Please write your honest reviews and experience of reading dark side of startup. You can also get a chance to meet personally with famous youtuber Mr. Arvind Arora (A2 Sir) and could also get a chance to win a signed copy from him.

You can also share your views on the email id : thedarksideofstartups@gmail.com

# Taking funding from the wrong investor in a Startup

# 8

Its seem like everyone might think that we got tired of writing and ended up choosing a wrong headline... but let us assure you that this isn't the case. We are still writing about our real experiences with complete honesty, so that we can convey to you all the things we want to actually convey through this book. Just like the title suggests, taking funding from the wrong investor, is this really such an important subject? Should a founder think about whom they're taking investment from, or should they just focus on the investment amount? You might be wondering how one can think of choosing an investor when it's the investor who is putting his hard earned money on stake. Can we allow being choosers even when the need is urgent?

Causing great confusion.......... Okay come

analysis this with us……

In our opinion, an investor in a startup is like an angel, nurturing the startup and leading it to greater heights. However, searching for that angel investor is also no less than a significant challenge. When you are into a startup, it is important to understand that making an investment is a risky call. It is possible that the entire invested amount might go in vain. Or maybe they end up earning 100 percent profit. Each startup founder is aware of the fact that not every startup is going to be a hit. If you are convincing an investor to put funds in your company, it is important for you to understand their mindset. Have they invested before? Because if they are aware of the risk of investments, you don't have to worry but if they do not have a good understanding of making an investment, it might cause you some trouble. If your startup wouldn't be able to generate profitable returns as per their expectations, it may pose some issues. A lot of startups and founders have gone through a similar situation, where they accepted small investments from investors, who did not have an investor's mindset. This was the reason behind the trouble they had to face later. At times these investors, just for the sake of having their money back, do not let the founders work. A lot of investors misbehave with founders which hinders their work capabilities and eventually, the startup has to suffer badly.

A similar story unfolded for a startup that raised 3 crore rupees by obtaining funds from around 40 individuals. Most of these investors were from the middle class. It was their first time investing, and everyone knew that the startup had immense potential in the coming times. Since the startup was already generating revenue, why would anyone ignore the opportunity to be a part of its promising journey? In this manner, everyone contributed based on their capacity, whether it was 1 lakh rupees or 10 lakhs rupees. Everyone was content, as creating an investor profile was a joyful task for some, and making the funding successful was a source of happiness for the founders.

However, fate had different plans. Just as beginnings are often auspicious, the same held true here. The founders worked diligently, and the investors were pleased. The founders kept the investors updated about the company's growth, and initially, the startup's sales were strong, and there was an abundance of funds. No problems seemed to be on the horizon.

But a few months later, disputes arose between the founders, and the entire story took a turn.

One of the founders has left the company, who was an expert in sales. Now, the entire burden of the company fell solely on this one founder.

They believed they could manage everything, but it didn't turn out that way. The company's sales started to decline, and expenses were increasing. The company's funds were depleting rapidly, and the founder's worry was growing.

Amidst this situation, some investors got wind of the company's deteriorating condition. They began discussing the possibility of withdrawing their investment from the company with the founder. At such times, you can imagine how troublesome this situation could be. What happened afterward... we don't think we need to explain.

Well, it's not important for us to know what ultimately happened to that company. What's important to understand is that behind making a startup successful, having the right investors plays a crucial role. Similarly, in the downfall of a startup, the role of investors can be significant, especially when you've taken money from the wrong investor. Now, before seeking investment, it's essential to have a clear understanding within yourself that choosing the right investors is crucial.

# Disputes between co-founders

# 9

We have all heard the saying that "two swords cannot be kept in one scabbard." Disputes among co-founders are quite common in startup companies. There can be several reasons behind conflicts between co-founders. In our view, disputes between co-founders could stem from ego clashes, one founder not dedicating enough attention to their role in the startup, differences in the company's vision among co-founders, one founder neglecting the contributions of the other founder, one founder exerting excessive control over the company and overshadowing the other founder's input, and outsiders provoking conflicts between the founders. Generally, these are the reasons that contribute to the escalation of disputes between co-founders. Similar situations have also arisen in several unicorn startups.

In our opinion, in a startup, founders should work in accordance with a founders' agreement.

The need for a founders' agreement generally arises when there's a problem or issue between the founders. A founders' agreement can encompass all the rules and conditions concerning the startup company, ensuring the protection of each founder's individual interests. This legal document outlines the terms and responsibilities of each founder, helping to prevent conflicts and disputes down the line. It's a crucial step to establish a clear understanding and alignment among co-founders from the very beginning.

Many times, founders encounter significant challenges when it comes to exiting a startup, either voluntarily or involuntarily. A founders' agreement becomes highly valuable in such situations. However, there are instances where founders misuse the founders' agreement and unethically use it as a means to remove other founders. Therefore, before signing a founders' agreement, it's crucial for all parties involved to carefully read and understand all the terms and conditions, ensuring that no problems arise in the future as a result of the agreement. Misusing such an agreement can lead to damaging consequences for the startup and the relationships among its founders.

A founders' agreement is one of the most crucial agreements that every startup's founders should consider. It's a contract created by the founders, which defines their business relationship. This agreement outlines the roles, responsibilities, and rights of the founders. Nowadays, startups have become highly popular among the youth, but the journey of a startup can be filled with challenges and uncertainties.

A founders' agreement is typically crafted to protect the interests of the founders. It establishes a clear framework for how the founders will work together, make decisions, allocate responsibilities, and handle potential disputes. This agreement becomes especially important as it helps prevent conflicts and misunderstandings among founders, ensuring a smoother journey for the startup through the complexities of its growth.

The primary purpose of a founders' agreement is to ensure that all founders work towards the startup's vision and goals. This agreement provides a legal framework for the startup, helping to clarify how the founders will manage and operate the startup. Without a founders' agreement, there is a risk of disputes among the founders, which can have detrimental effects on the success of the startup.

The founders' agreement outlines various aspects, such as equity distribution, decision-making processes, roles and responsibilities, contributions, intellectual property ownership, vesting schedules, and more. By addressing these matters in advance, the agreement helps in preventing misunderstandings and conflicts that could potentially arise as the startup grows.

Overall, a well-drafted founders' agreement serves as a crucial tool to ensure alignment among founders and provides a solid foundation for the startup's growth and success.

It's highly advisable to have a legal advisor review your founders' agreement, as their expertise can help mitigate potential issues that may arise in the future. When signing a founders' agreement, everyone tends to have positive interactions and a shared goal of propelling the startup forward. There's usually a sense of happiness and excitement, and due to this, individuals might overlook the specific terms and conditions that could have a significant impact on their hard work in the future.

The intention behind this discussion is not to be negative, but rather to encourage vigilance. We've come across several startups where no trace of a founders' agreement exists. Verbal commitments alone may seem sufficient, but legally they often don't hold up. Seeking legal counsel can ensure that your startup is built on a solid foundation, and potential conflicts or uncertainties can be avoided with a well-crafted founders' agreement.

Indeed, conflicts among founders within a startup company have led to the downfall of several promising and potentially profitable ventures. This represents a dark side of startups that can lead to their demise. Disagreements among founders can have serious implications, often resulting in a lack of alignment, compromised decision-making, and a strained working relationship. The expertise and skills necessary for the startup's success might become inaccessible due to the founders' discord.

Not only founders, but even investors can also suffer from these internal disputes. When the startup's core team is embroiled in conflicts, it can affect their ability to meet commitments, achieve milestones, and attract additional funding. The growth trajectory of the startup can be severely impacted, leading to financial losses for both founders and investors.

It's crucial for startup founders to recognize the potential consequences of unresolved disputes and take proactive steps to address and manage conflicts. Establishing a clear and well-documented founders' agreement, open communication channels, and a strong conflict resolution process can contribute in maintaining a healthy startup ecosystem and increasing the chances of long-term success.

"The Founders knew that uncontrolled power is always dangerous. No person or group is immune from mistakes, selfishness and greed."

# Choosing the Wrong Consultant for a Startup

# 10

"In the journey of a startup company, from its inception to becoming a unicorn or even until its closure, there are significant roles played by individuals other than the founders. These include the senior management, senior employees, as well as legal and financial consultants associated with the company. Many times, the wrong selection of advisors early in the startup's journey can lead to the emergence of non-compliance issues. This becomes evident when the company undergoes the due diligence process while seeking to raise funds. Some startups face challenges in securing funding even after completing a funding round, due to negative findings in their due diligence reports.

The due diligence report often serves as an eye-opener for many startup founders, highlighting where and how their legal and financial consultants may have made mistakes. Legal and financial consultants possess a comprehensive understanding of both the positive and negative aspects of your startup. They act as facilitators as long as their personal and professional interests remain aligned with the company's objectives. However, when startup founders decide to replace these consultants with new ones, issues such as the poor behavior and other problems caused by the previous consultants can arise.

"To avoid such problems for startup founders, it's crucial to always make the right choices when selecting the company's legal and financial consultants, as well as senior employees. This ensures that founders do not have to endure such challenges. Making the right selection is essential to prevent such situations from arising in the journey of a startup."

Startup founders typically come from technical backgrounds, which often means they have limited knowledge about legal and financial matters. Their reliance on legal and financial advisors is quite high due to this lack of expertise. If a mistake occurs, it can be difficult to identify for them, and here lies one of the biggest pitfalls that founders may have to face. It's always the founders who bear the consequences of such mistakes. It's essential for founders to have a grasp of legal and financial aspects. Additionally, founders can consider having a personal alternative as a second opinion for legal and financial matters, so that potential major errors can be avoided before they happen.

Numerous non-compliance issues often surface within a startup company, such as non-compliances in the share allotment process, income tax and GST-related non-compliances, non-compliances related to share transfers, non-compliances in company-related filings, and non-compliances in ESOPs implementation. Startup founders should ensure periodic check-ups of the company's financial health. These checks can help in identifying potential non-compliance issues and rectifying them in a timely manner.

We came across something similar in a Bangalore-based startup, where the founders assigned the responsibility of handling all the financial and legal matters of their company to an advisor. The founders had a technical background and did not understand financial and legal matters. In such a situation, their complete reliance was on that advisor. The founders of the company first rose funding of 2 crore rupees from investors. The advisor ensured that all the compliances for the investment were met according to his calculations. After that, the company's founders raised another 1 crore rupee investment two months later, at a valuation twice the initial valuation. The company also received the money from the second investment round into its account.

Until then, everything was going well, and the company was also performing well. Now, the founders of the company were raising the next funding round from a major Venture Capital (VC) firm. The VC firm also prepared to invest in the company and a Term Sheet was signed with the company. After committing to invest, the VC firm began its due diligence process on the company. The founders of the company received a major shock when the VC firm decided not to provide funding during the due diligence process. The founders couldn't understand what had suddenly happened that caused the VC firm to step back from the investment deal.

The founders learned from internal sources of the VC firm that due to significant deficiencies in the company's accounting, financials, and documentation systems, the VC firm decided not to proceed with the deal. This situation is quite unbearable for any startup founder, to see a large funding round being halted for some reason. Now the company engaged another consultancy firm to conduct a due diligence process, in order to understand where things were going wrong. Meanwhile, the previous advisor who was working with the company declined to continue working with them in the future. Now, the founders were starting to realize that there were indeed some issues with the company's compliance.

When the founders of the company looked at their company's due diligence report, they discovered numerous non-compliances that posed significant challenges for the company. Although it's difficult to say why the VC firm stepped back from the investment deal, the founders found many mistakes made by their previous advisor. The documents created during the first funding round were incomplete, and there were many non-compliances in the allocation of shares in the company. Even after receiving funds from some investors, shares were not allocated to them, and due to fear of being caught, the company showed those funds as sales and paid GST on them.

In the subsequent funding round, investments were received, but the allocation of shares for that investment was not done either. In this manner, several non-compliances within the company were revealed during that due diligence process. Now you must understand how the wrong choices of an advisor can lead a company and its founders to face significant problems.

Many times, due to the advice of the

company's advisors, the founders make mistakes, and then those advisors also exert pressure on them. Because of this, the founders are unable to remove these advisors from the company. In this way, wrong advisors become a problem for the company, and these advisors hinder the company's growth due to their personal interests. This is a dark side that is observed in many startups.

**Team Efforts goes vain when your Consultant's effort is in wrong direction.**

## To issue shares under the name 'Advisory Shares' to reduce the valuation for a specific individual

# 11

When a startup needs to provide leverage to specific investors, it is done in the form of advisory shares. You can think of this as transferring a certain number of shares from the founder's own shares to an investor without requiring a monetary investment, and an advisory agreement is established. These investors are brought onto the company's CAP Table, with a crucial role to play in the company's growth. However, besides these advisory shares, investors also make some monetary investments in the company. For this, the company allocates shares against the investment amount, similar to how it does for other investors.

Looking at this from another perspective, it could indeed be a simple way of allocating shares to a specific individual at a lower valuation than other investors. However, we are not entirely opposed to this idea, but we believe that other investors should have a sufficient understanding of this arrangement. Your point is valid that adequate comprehension of this exchange is essential for other investors so they can grasp the situation and understand the implications of their investments.

Such practices can be complex in both social and financial contexts, so using sound judgment and utilizing strategies wisely is crucial.

Generally, in startups, advisory shares are usually granted to a specific individual in the range of 0.5% to 1%. However, these days, in small startups, shares under the name of advisory shares are transferred to a particular individual at times exceeding 10%, and sometimes even more. In this scenario, it doesn't seem logical to grant such a significant amount of advisory shares in a startup. Many startups use this as a tool to provide equity to new investors at par with or even less than the valuation of old investors. It's often utilized as a leverage point so that new investors can receive equity equivalent to or less than that of existing investors.

Here you may note that equity distribution and practices can vary widely and are influenced by various factors including the startup's funding needs, growth prospects, and negotiation dynamics with investors.

Now you might be wondering about the benefits for startup founders from doing this. There are two advantages for startup founders. The first advantage is that startups receive new investments without diminishing the valuation in the eyes of existing investors.

By utilizing advisory shares in this manner, startups can effectively attract new investments while maintaining their perceived valuation stability among the current investors. This approach can be strategic in managing the delicate balance between funding needs and the perception of the company's worth by stakeholders.

**Let's understand this with an example:**

"Extraordinary Private Limited," a startup, obtained an investment of ₹50 lakh from Ravi Malhotra in the year 2022 at a valuation of ₹10 crore. In 2023, the company needed new investments, but its performance was not on par with its previous valuation. The founders of the company didn't want to reveal this to Ravi Malhotra. At that time, another investor, Pawan Manchanda, was ready to invest ₹25 lakh in the company. However, he was only willing to invest at a valuation of ₹5 crore.

The founders knew that Ravi Malhotra, who had initially invested at a valuation of ₹10 crore, wouldn't agree to invest at a lower valuation. So, the founders presented Pawan Manchanda as an expert advisor to the company, transferring a percentage of shares to him at a valuation that was acceptable to both parties. This allowed Pawan Manchanda to have a stake in the company, compensating for the lower valuation, while Ravi Malhotra's investment remained unaffected. And they obtained consent from them for advisory shares. Now, the founders allocated 2.5% of equity, valuing 10 crore, in exchange for a 2.5 lakh investment to the new investor and provided 2.5% of equity in the form of advisory shares. In this manner, the new investor effectively invested at a valuation of 5 crore.

Please note that the equity distribution and valuation changes in this example are for illustrative purposes and may not represent actual market conditions. The example demonstrates the concept of using advisory shares to align investor interests and manage equity allocation creatively. In this way, the startup managed to secure new investment without affecting its overall valuation and without revealing its current performance to the existing investor.

This example demonstrates how advisory shares can be strategically used to navigate investment challenges and maintain investor confidence.

## To increase expensive spaces and excessive staff in the desire for showmanship and quick growth

# 12

The current situation is quite unusual, something we've observed with many startups. When founders successfully close their funding rounds for their startups, the first thing they usually focus on is marketing. After that initial euphoria of securing funding, the company's business takes a back seat for a few days, and the founders start promoting themselves like marketing themselves as the face of the company. They go around giving talks, attending startup events, and sharing their experiences as speakers.

We believe a true entrepreneur is someone who first makes their startup successful. Just raising funds doesn't guarantee a startup's success. Many founders lose their focus after securing funding, thinking that their team will take care of things going forward. They end up wasting their time on self-promotion. Startup founders need to understand here that their biggest marketing asset is the success of their startup.

After securing funding, the expenses and extravagance of many startup founders tend to increase significantly. Companies tend to hire more employees than necessary. For the company, a large space in a big corporate park is rented at a high cost. All kinds of unnecessary expenses might seem evident at that time, but founders often don't pay much attention to these at the beginning. Their hearts and minds are focused on branding and marketing during that time, and if they have the money, why would anyone think otherwise?

This is the right time when you can lead the company towards a sustainable business model by utilizing funds wisely, enabling the company to grow substantially. However, such maturity is not often seen among most startup founders. And where this maturity is evident, those startups tend to succeed in moving forward.

A similar Edtech startup company began its journey from Mumbai in 2018. The founders of the startup had a five-year experience working in Edtech unicorns as Vice Presidents. With their strong background and experience, raising investment wasn't challenging for them. The company secured an initial funding of 10 crore INR. Initially, the company focused on building a technology platform, content, and assembling a competent team, which were the right decisions considering the startup phase.

The company witnessed good sales traction early on, receiving positive responses due to its unique selling proposition (USP). Building on this success, the company raised an additional funding of 20 crore INR during the COVID-19 pandemic. This marks the beginning of the competition in the unicorn Edtech space.

The company then focused on building its marketing and brand image, enhancing the founders' public relations efforts, opening an office in a large and prestigious location, and establishing offices in more than 10 cities for extensive sales and marketing activities.

The founders focused solely on bringing in funding, which led them to hire more employees and increase other expenses within the company. The startup's spending was aligned with the assumption that the need for reinvestment would arise soon, given the rate at which they were spending. Now, the pressure was on the founders to secure new investments, as the startup's metrics had deteriorated to a point where securing funds in such circumstances was not easy. As funds dwindled, the company started to cut costs by closing offices in certain cities and layoffs.

Unfortunately, not long after, due to a complete depletion of funds within the startup, the founders made the difficult decision to shut down the company. At that point, the company's 200 employees had not received salaries for two months. The platform on which the company had sold courses was no longer operational as the company hadn't paid for services like AWS (Amazon Web Services) and other online portals. Both the employees and customers of the company were adversely affected, leading to frustration and disappointment towards the founders.

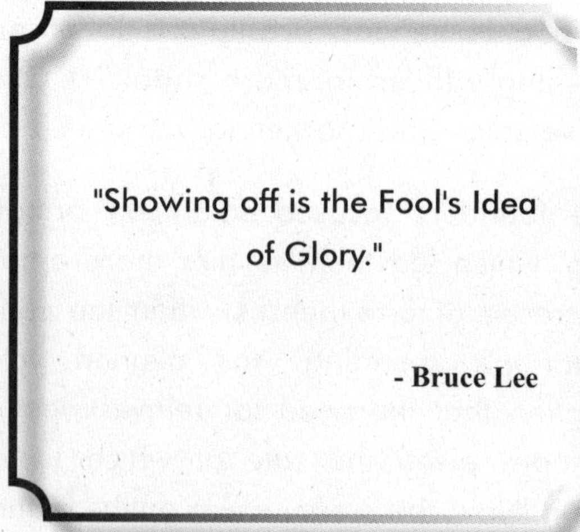

"Showing off is the Fool's Idea of Glory."

- **Bruce Lee**

# Improper utilization of funds in a Startup

# 13

We have observed many startup founders and noticed changes in their behavior. Their behavior tends to be quite distinct when they are not receiving funding, when they secure funding, and after the funding has been depleted. However, we view this change in behavior as a part of human nature, as it is a natural process that often unfolds.

Obtaining funding in a startup is not an easy task; you need to pitch the right business to the right investors. The funding process involves several stages even after pitching. Typically, it takes at least two months to secure funding. Before securing funding, founders often spend their funds judiciously, as they are aware that if funding doesn't come through, they will have to sustain the company in the long run with their own resources.

When a company receives funding from investors, certain things change for the founders. For instance, there is an increased emphasis on rapidly scaling the company, boosting its topline (turnover) It can be challenging to secure funding in a startup as you need to pitch the right business to the right investors. The funding process involves multiple stages even after the initial pitch. Generally, it takes at least two months to secure funding. Before securing funding, founders judiciously manage their funds because they understand that if funding doesn't materialize, they'll need to keep the company afloat using their own resources.

When a company secures funding, founders often need to make several decisions. These decisions can include mass hiring, creating an organizational structure, planning for sales and marketing, developing or upgrading the company's tech platform, and building a larger infrastructure. Among these decisions, the biggest risk often lies in the misuse of investment funds. In many instances, startups have been observed to offer inexperienced employees higher salaries, leading to mismanagement of investor funds.

Additionally, after receiving funds, founders' spending often increases for items such as travel costs, event expenses, and consulting fees. Some startups tend to allocate excessive budgets for marketing and branding promotions, surpassing even their sales expenditures. As a result, customer acquisition costs rise substantially. Today, even unicorn startups are not immune to misusing investor funds. They sometimes use investor funds to sponsor significant events in the country. However, it's a different matter whether such sponsorships genuinely benefit the startup or if they're simply for show and founders' enjoyment.

We believe this is a topic that warrants thoughtful consideration."

When investors' funds are misused, that's usually when preparations to secure new funding begin. Now, when seeking new funds, it becomes essential to increase the company's valuation, which often requires growing the company's topline...Indeed, after the misuse of funds, the remaining funds are often strategically utilized to position the company for securing new funding. This involves allocating resources in a way that demonstrates growth to new potential investors, making the company appealing for new investment.

Absolutely, if you find yourself making these mistakes as a startup founder, it's crucial to take a step back and refrain from misusing the company's funds for short-term gains. Instead, consider how you can use these funds to scale the company and build a sustainable business. It's essential for founders to utilize investor funds in a prudent manner, just as they do with their own funds. Failing to do so could jeopardize not only the company's future with investors but also your own growth and career. This is indeed one of the darker sides of the startup world that every founder should be aware of.

> *"Rule No. 1 is never lose money. Rule No. 2 is never forget Rule No. 1."*
>
> **- Warren Buffett**

# Continuing the investments rounds despite of ongoing losses in a Startup

## 14

Approximately 80% of the country's unicorn startups are still not profitable. This startup ecosystem has evolved in such a way that profitability isn't a necessity for a startup's valuation, serving as a benchmark for founders. A company's valuation depends on various factors. Even startups that have been operating at a loss since inception hold the hope that one day they can turn their startup into a unicorn. It's in this hope that startups continue to incur losses while enhancing their valuation alongside other factors. Now, if funding continues to flow in, you can keep playing the funding rounds and eventually turn your company into a unicorn. However, if funding dries up before or after achieving unicorn status, you have three options. The first option is to arrange a buyout for your company. The second option is to go for an IPO (Initial Public Offering) for your company. The third option is for the company to shut down.

The fun part is that from starting a startup to becoming a unicorn and even after becoming a unicorn, there is no shortage of risks for you. However, amidst all this, you receive a decent salary from the company, which keeps your survival worries at bay. Real money is made when your paths open up for the first option or the second option. Now, you must have understood why startup founders take the risk of running a startup at a loss. Out of the 100 percent startups in the country, only around half a percent (even less than 1 percent) of startups manage to reach a good level. For most startup founders, their careers and futures are put on the line because even after their startups fail to secure funding, maintaining their startup through bank loans or personal funds is akin to facing suicide. Additionally, the precious time of founders is consumed, during which they could have achieved financial stability for themselves and their families. This is the dark side of startups, often unseen by founders in the beginning, but as they sink deeper into the mire of losses, they gradually realize its depth.

An FMCG startup company with a valuation exceeding 100 crore faced closure within a year after failing to secure further funding from investors. This story belongs to three founders from IIT Mumbai. They invested their most valuable time into building this startup and eventually, the company is now undergoing the Corporate Insolvency Resolution Process (IRP), indicating its closure. Today, these three founders are working in separate companies, seeking a better life away from the problems of the startup. The story of this FMCG startup is quite intriguing, and we will share it with you. This story will also help you understand how the ups and downs in a startup impact your personal life.

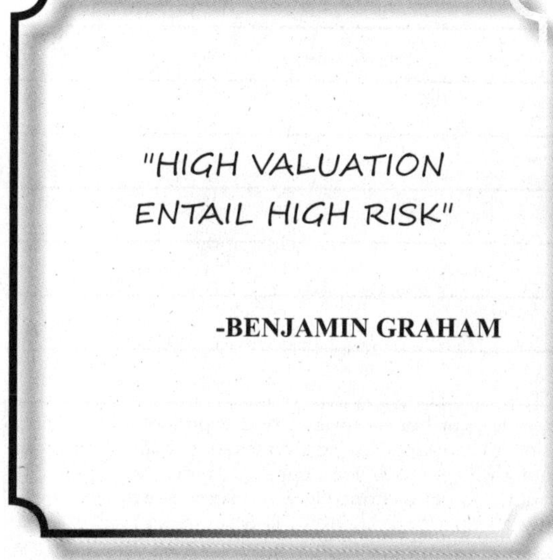

## "THE DARKSIDE OF STARTUPS"

**YOUR THOUGHTS ON DARK SIDES OF STARTUPS**

Name :

Contact Number :

CHAPTER REVIEW NOTE -2

Please write your honest reviews and experience of reading dark side of startup. You can also get a chance to meet personally with famous youtuber Mr. Arvind Arora (A2 Sir) and could also get a chance to win a signed copy from him.

**You can also share your views on the email id : thedarksideofstartups@gmail.com**

# On the behest of investors, increasing the cash burn rate rapidly to boost topline valuation

# 15

This is a somewhat serious topic, and we believe that larger investors and VC firms should consider this carefully. The question here is about the future of many startup founders, who tirelessly work day and night to make their startup successful, fueled by the belief in their hard work. However, due to the greed of investors, they often end up getting ahead in the race so much that they don't even realize that the investors have moved on to something else. When such a situation is observed with a startup, it's truly disheartening.

Let's understand this - the game of investment in a startup is entirely based on valuation. As far as my understanding goes, the biggest factor affecting valuation is a company's turnover, referred to as the "topline". This means that as a company's turnover increases, its valuation also goes up. And as the company's valuation grows, it moves closer to becoming a unicorn. Investors put money into startups primarily to capitalize on the benefits of the startup's increasing valuation. This is where they make substantial profits.

Investors are well aware that while they might invest in 100 startups, if even one of those startups becomes a unicorn, their investment will yield returns. Now the question arises, what about the others?

**Certainly, let's understand it through cases:**

**Case – 1** The founders of an FMCG startup were graduates from IIT Mumbai. Their product was exceptional, with packaging being the main unique selling point (USP). Starting with an initial investment of 1 crore, they later raised 10 crores. The startup's turnover was around 5 crores in the early stages. The product was available in modern trade stores, with sales coming through various channels. The company's repeat orders were strong, and it even exported its food products to Gulf countries. It had managed to secure listings with major airlines.

Before facing its end, the startup managed to secure a final funding round of 40 crores from a Mauritius-based VC firm.

The founders were steering the startup in the right direction. Investors were pleased with the company's growth. The founders were confident in their growth and margins. The founders were also investing in other startups. While investors emphasized increasing the topline to enhance valuation, the founders were focused on sustainable growth and preparing for listing within the next 2-3 years.

During the Series A round, the startup was approached by a Mauritius-based VC firm ready to invest over 100 crores in future rounds. According to investors, if the founders were capable of accelerating revenue through controlled cash burn, the concern about cash burn should be secondary, as the VC firm was willing to invest more than 40 crores in the future.

However, the company's systematic growth shifted towards enhancing valuation. Cash was invested in marketing, branding, and team expansion. Nearly 40 crores were burned in 18 months, as they anticipated further funding rounds.

Unfortunately, the VC firm's commitment wavered, and it chose to invest 120 crores in another startup following a similar pattern, which is now a unicorn. This sudden shift left the founders in a difficult position. They managed to secure funding from other sources, but the financial pressure started impacting marketing and branding efforts.

With the founders' dedication and a personal guarantee on debt funding, they managed to keep the company afloat. However, a founder had to leave due to personal financial commitments, and another left due to family pressure. Only one founder remained, with the responsibility of running the company.

After months of hard work, the remaining founder faced difficulties in timely vendor payments, leading the startup towards insolvency and bankruptcy. The once-promising startup's founders are now working for different MNCs, moving forward with their lives, leaving behind the trials and tribulations of their previous venture.

This narrative serves as a poignant reminder of the challenges startups face and the resilience required to navigate the volatile startup landscape.

**Case - 2**: The Rise, Fall, and Resilience of TechFin Startup

## Introduction:

XYZ TechFin was a promising startup that aimed to revolutionize the financial technology landscape. Founded by three tech-savvy entrepreneurs who had graduated from top universities, the company sought to bridge the gap between technology and finance. With innovative solutions and a dynamic team, they embarked on their journey with a vision to transform the industry.

## Early Success and Investment:

The startup began with an initial seed funding of $1 million, which enabled them to develop a cutting-edge platform that seamlessly integrated financial services into users' everyday lives. Their product gained traction rapidly due to its user-friendly interface and value-added services. Within a short span, they secured a Series A funding of $10 million, propelling them to expand their operations.

## Innovative Products and Strategic Partnerships:

The startup's unique selling point (USP) was its ability to offer personalized financial solutions based on users' behavior and preferences. They introduced a range of products, from investment advisory to automated savings, attracting a diverse user base. Strategic partnerships with major financial institutions lent credibility to their offerings and fostered trust among users.

## Growth and Challenges:

As the startup's user base grew, so did their ambitions. They expanded their product line and introduced premium subscription models. The company's valuation soared, and investors poured in substantial funding to fuel their growth. However, this growth trajectory was not without challenges. Regulatory hurdles, operational complexities, and competition from established players tested the founders' resolve.

## Investor Expectations and Pressure:

Investors began to emphasize rapid revenue growth, expecting the startup to achieve higher valuation milestones. The founders faced increasing pressure to scale operations and customer acquisition, sometimes at the expense of profitability. The once-idealistic startup was now navigating the fine line between maintaining its vision and meeting investor demands.

## Shift in Focus and Consequences:

In response to investor expectations, the startup shifted its focus from customer-centric innovation to aggressive expansion. Cash burn rates increased significantly as they targeted uncharted markets and launched high-budget marketing campaigns. While their user base continued to grow, the startup's financials started showing signs of strain.

## Sudden Turn of Events:

During a pivotal funding round, one of their key investors unexpectedly backed out due to market uncertainties. This left the startup scrambling to secure funding from alternative sources. The situation worsened as competitors introduced similar offerings, intensifying the battle for market share.

## Resilience and Hard Choices:

Facing financial constraints, the startup's founders had to make tough decisions. They implemented cost-cutting measures, reduced staff, and scaled back marketing campaigns. Despite the challenges, the founders remained committed to their mission, focusing on improving the platform's efficiency and refining their core products.

## Lessons Learned:

The TechFin startup's journey highlights the delicate balance between investor expectations and maintaining a sustainable growth trajectory. While funding is crucial, startups should prioritize maintaining their core vision and sound financial practices. The ability to adapt to changing circumstances, make difficult decisions, and focus on delivering value to customers is essential for long-term success.

## Conclusion:

The XYZ TechFin startup's story serves as a case study on the challenges startups face in managing investor pressure, sustaining growth, and adapting to a dynamic market. While the startup encountered setbacks and hurdles, the founders' resilience, adaptability, and commitment to their vision allowed them to weather the storm and emerge stronger. This case underscores the importance of a well-rounded approach to growth and the need for startups to stay true to their core values, even in the face of adversity.

> **Manager And Investors Alike Must Understand That Accounting Numbers Are The Beginning, Not The End On Business Valuation.**
>
> **- Warren Buffett**

# Using a lot of funding in the wrong business model of a company.

# 16

The current situation is such that startup founders are in a rush to scale their startups in the race to become unicorns. In this haste, they quickly hire new people, develop new products and launch them in the market, enter new markets without proper research, and secure significant funding at high valuations. It might surprise you that despite doing all this, over 70% of startups end up failing.

A major reason for a startup's failure is often the rush to scale rapidly without a proper understanding of the initial phase. Many times, startups with flawed business models try to scale quickly and end up using most of their funding to scale. By the time they realize their business model is flawed, a substantial portion of the company's funds has been exhausted.

There are numerous startups founded by individuals from prestigious institutions like IIT and IIM who have witnessed this situation up close. We often remain optimistic about our product, service, and business model, hoping to succeed in acquiring customers.

Indeed, sometimes that is the case. It's not necessary, and when it doesn't happen, we put all our effort into acquiring customers at any cost. This effort can sometimes lead founders to drain their resources like water, relentlessly pouring money to acquire customers. Even today, you'll find examples of startups that are willing to spend up to 200 rupees to extract 1 rupee from a customer. In your view, you might even call this behavior irrational, but it's the harsh reality of the startup world.

This practice might seem wasteful, but it's a dark and bitter truth of the startup ecosystem.

> **"Luck is not a Business Model"**
>
> **Anthony Bourdain**

## Focusing more on marketing and branding rather than the quality of the core product or service

# 17

After most startups get funding, they lose their focus and cannot understand what their purpose was behind creating the startup. Forgetting all of this, they try to market their company and product/service only as a brand. Due to this, they lose their focus. When a startup has multiple products/services, they should concentrate on a main product/service and work on improving its quality. This ensures that no other product/service or brand can compete with it in the market. This is what gives your startup its Unique Selling Proposition (USP) in the market. Developing a high-quality product/service is better than entering the market with several average-quality products/services.

## "THE DARKSIDE OF STARTUPS"

## YOUR THOUGHTS ON DARK SIDES OF STARTUPS

Name :

Contact Number :

CHAPTER REVIEW NOTE -3

Please write your honest reviews and experience of reading dark side of startup. You can also get a chance to meet personally with famous youtuber Mr. Arvind Arora (A2 Sir) and could also get a chance to win a signed copy from him.

**You can also share your views on the email id : thedarksideofstartups@gmail.com**

# Securing funding based on inflated valuations by showing false growth to investors

# 18

The startup world has a dark reality that the entire game of startups has become a way to benefit investors more than business. Early-stage investors give funding to startups at a certain valuation, and that valuation increases along with the startup's topline (Revenue/Sales). This allows the startup to keep receiving new funding at the increasing valuation. Meanwhile, some investors exit at the right time while new investors enter the game at this valuation.

The problem arises when a company reaches a level where its performance starts declining or its funding begins to deplete. This leads to a drop in the company's topline, and at that point, founders often make decisions without careful consideration about whether the company should continue growing or stay at the same level. This is where many startups resort to dishonest practices to inflate their valuation. They manipulate their topline by creating fake revenue/sales or using leftover funds to show genuine growth.

In doing so, startups try to attract new investors by artificially inflating their valuations. This behavior is driven by the pressure to keep up appearances, maintain high valuations, and secure further funding. It's essential for founders to consider the long-term consequences of such actions and focus on building sustainable growth based on genuine performance and value creation.

If a startup has reached such a situation, its eventual demise is inevitable, and startup founders must understand this fact. Investors usually don't incur losses primarily because even if they lose money in one place, they are likely making profits elsewhere. The most significant struggle here is for startup founders and the employees working in those startups. Such startups are creating a bubble in the country, which will eventually end the careers of many founders and potentially leave numerous employees unemployed.

# siphoning of funds from company in a non- compliant manner for discretionary use

# 19

Startups often experience internal disagreements among founders, usually related to mismanagement of company funds. Accusations of deception are directed towards founders who withdraw funds from the company. Similarly, investors in startups also frequently level such allegations against founders. This scenario has been observed in numerous startups. Recently, even a unicorn startup founder has faced similar accusations. Misusing funds is a separate issue from wrongfully extracting funds from the company, which is another matter altogether.

Firstly, let's understand the situation of investors' funds being squandered by founders. In several startups, investor funds are misused extensively, such as hiring more employees than necessary, allocating money to different individuals for the same task, inflating office expenses, and spending on marketing and branding. The mismanagement of funds in any startup is usually a result of weak management, impulsive decision-making, and inadequate internal control.

Startup founders can prevent this if they wish.

Now let's understand the situation of founders misusing investor funds. In many startups, founders intentionally or with wrong intentions use company funds for personal gain. This is referred to as fund misappropriation or misusing funds for personal benefit. You can think of this as a form of fraud on a smaller scale, and it's considered an offensive action. It is an unethical act for startup founders, which goes against the interests of both the company and the investors. As an example, if any startup founder incurs personal expenses not approved by the company and still uses company funds for such expenses, it is considered unethical.

Lastly, let's talk about the most serious issue, where startup founders illicitly cash out investors' funds from the company through unauthorized means. This is the gravest concern in the startup world. It's known as "siphoning of funds." There are instances where startup founders have withdrawn money from the company through fraudulent bills, contracts, and by using fake employees' names. Recently, a unicorn startup's founder faced legal action due to unauthorized fund withdrawal. There have been cases where founders have dismantled old startups in this way and used the same money to start new ventures, running their new startups without funding. This brings me to a clear understanding that when an investor funds a startup, it's crucial to assess the founder's intent.

Remember, the intent of the founder matters significantly when investors decide to fund a startup.

Startup founders need to understand that they should not even entertain the idea of engaging in unethical activities. Any form of illegal action could destroy their careers. Nowadays, everyone is aware that there is no bigger court of public opinion than social media in this country. In today's era, what is visible is what gets attention. Currently, startup founders pay so much attention to their personal branding that they have the power to suppress their unethical actions with their personal branding. Additionally, there are many startup founders who, even after engaging in unethical activities, manage to become celebrities in the eyes of the public.

*Your reputation is more important than your paycheck, and your integrity is worth more than your career.*

**– Ryan Freitas**

# Reality of Unicorn Startup or Bad Startup

## 20

These days, there's a surge of large-scale startups in the country, but you might be surprised to learn that this is contributing to some serious issues as well. These startups, in order to expand their market, offer their products/services to customers at very low prices by utilizing investor funds. This has led to the downfall of previously profitable small-scale businesses, as they lack the financial backing from investors. These local businesses cannot afford to market their products/services effectively, either too little or too much, due to budget constraints.

Consequently, many previously profitable small businesses are on the brink of shutting down. Several startups have diverted the funds from investors not towards growing their own business, but instead towards undermining their competitors. This phenomenon is particularly evident in the large and unicorn edtech startups. When the funding for these major startups starts to dry up, thousands of people simultaneously find themselves unemployed, and among them, there are many who were handed jobs with extremely high salaries to intentionally cause harm to other companies.

This complex situation reflects the interplay between the growth of big startups, the challenges faced by local businesses, the competition-driven strategies of certain startups, and the consequences of funding shortages. It's a dynamic landscape that impacts both the startup ecosystem and the broader economy.

Most of the major startups, by misusing investor funds, offer extravagant salaries to the workforce and management of stable businesses, thereby luring them into jobs. In this manner, these startups undermine other stable businesses for their own benefit. Although these startups may initially benefit, their actions continuously erode business ethics. Due to their unethical competition and hostile strategies, big startups sometimes end up disrupting potential startups.

Several startup founders have managed to create personal assets by unethically diverting investor funds. Some founders have misused funds to shut down their companies and then used that money to establish new startups. This is a very serious issue, a dark truth of the startup world that cannot be denied.

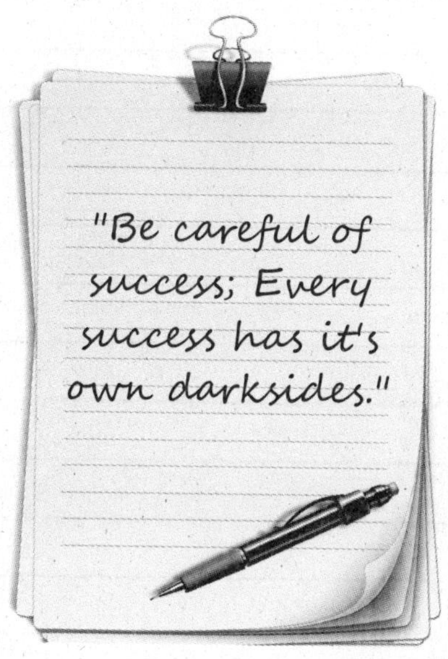

## "THE DARKSIDE OF STARTUPS"

## YOUR THOUGHTS ON DARK SIDES OF STARTUPS

Name :

Contact Number :

CHAPTER REVIEW NOTE -4

Please write your honest reviews and experience of reading dark side of startup. You can also get a chance to meet personally with famous youtuber Mr. Arvind Arora (A2 Sir) and could also get a chance to win a signed copy from him.

You can also share your views on the email id : thedarksideofstartups@gmail.com

# Taking a loan to save the Startup from shutting down

## 21

Recently, we attended an event where various loan schemes were being discussed for bank startup funding. Hearing about it felt really good because it seemed like banks are now supporting startups to move forward. During this time, when we heard questions from startup founders, we were amazed when we learned how a startup can choose options for taking a loan from the bank for a few months of runway (runway refers to the time until a startup receives new funding, during which they might consider taking a loan to keep running). You might find this strange too, but it's quite common in the startup world. When a startup's investment funds are exhausted and there's a delay in securing new funding or funding isn't available yet, startup founders take unsecured loans from banks to cover expenses for a few months and keep the company alive. Even after being in a loss, the company turns its books profitable and portrays those extra expenses as Intellectual Property work in progress, essentially showing them as assets in the company's books.

This enables the company to appear profitable and eligible for an unsecured loan from the bank. Some startups, even after incurring losses, take Investor's Debt Fund with a personal guarantee and against personal assets. Apart from bank loans, startups also have options for such Investor's Debt Fund that fund even loss-making startups. Such startups, which aren't easily funded by banks due to their losses, have an option to secure loans from Investor's Debt Fund. Debt Funds come in various forms, such as revenue-based (RBF) loans for startups.

Recently, a unicorn faced difficulties in closing an investment funding round, and for a few months, the company's expenses were managed through a Debt Fund. Imagine that if a company can't successfully close a funding round, the same might also face closure, especially if the company is already running at substantial losses that founders can't turn profitable even if they want to. During such times, unicorn founders are left with only the hope of securing new funding, and they are compelled to take steps driven by this hope.

The issue here is not whether a loan will be granted or not. The real issue is when and when not to take a loan in a startup. The right time to take a loan is when the company's return on investment is greater than the interest rate of the bank loan. When a company takes a loan from the bank, it's crucial for them to see if the loan amount, when invested in the business, generates more income than the interest costs. Now, if you think about startups incurring losses, you'll understand that for them, apart from the issue of losses, bank loans become problematic.

**"Small Loan makes a Debt; but a great one is enemy of Startup"**

## "THE DARKSIDE OF STARTUPS"

## YOUR THOUGHTS ON DARK SIDES OF STARTUPS

Name :

Contact Number :

CHAPTER REVIEW NOTE -5

Please write your honest reviews and experience of reading dark side of startup. You can also get a chance to meet personally with famous youtuber Mr. Arvind Arora (A2 Sir) and could also get a chance to win a signed copy from him.

**You can also share your views on the email id :**
**thedarksideofstartups@gmail.com**

# Exploiting retail investors in a Startup IPO for the benefit of founders and investors

# 22

In India, the startup IPO trend was thriving during a bullish market phase. The arrival of these IPOs generated a lot of excitement in the market and was seen as a new way of investment for many small investors. However, this trend abruptly slowed down, primarily because some of the most talked-about startups struggled upon getting listed on exchanges. Following this, a situation emerged where several startups delayed their plans for launching an IPO.

Understanding this game is quite straightforward. A startup begins, raises funding, increases its valuation, launches an IPO with an inflated valuation, shifts the losses onto the general public in the form of small investors, and eventually exits while keeping those investors who hoped for 10-20 times returns at bay. Founders take hefty salaries. Ultimately, by launching an IPO, selling most of their ownership at a good price, and providing small portions to individual investors, they make money. This way, in a few years, the startup's management undergoes changes to align with these goals.

It's important to note that not all startups follow such practices. There are ethical and responsible startups that prioritize the well-being of all stakeholders, including investors. When investing, it's crucial to research the company's history, management, financials, and overall business strategy. Additionally, regulatory bodies and market authorities play a role in ensuring fairness and transparency in IPOs and other investment activities.

It's true that some startup founders manage to detach themselves from their startups and create a lavish lifestyle. Whether the startup thrives or fails, the common people bear the brunt of the losses. The conclusion is that many startups have launched their IPOs despite running in losses, and we have witnessed the outcomes. All startup companies' shares are experiencing significant declines in the stock market. Ultimately, the losses were incurred by the retail investors who invested in these startups.

This is the harsh reality of many startups, where regular people have suffered losses in terms of crores (millions) of rupees as retail investors, while the startup founders and investors have secured their futures using the money of these ordinary individuals. This disparity highlights a significant issue in the startup world. While founders and investors profit from IPOs, retail investors, who often lack the same level of insight and expertise, are left facing financial losses.

Looking ahead, the path to IPOs might become more challenging for startups, as retail investors might become more cautious about investing in IPOs of startups that have a history of losses. The dynamics of startup IPOs could shift, and regulatory bodies might also become stricter to ensure greater transparency and fairness in these processes. It's important for both investors and startups to consider ethical and responsible practices to ensure a more balanced and sustainable growth ecosystem.

**"You didn't lose money in Startup's IPO, You paid for a lesson."**

## "THE DARKSIDE OF STARTUPS"

## YOUR THOUGHTS ON DARK SIDES OF STARTUPS

Name :

Contact Number :

CHAPTER REVIEW NOTE -6

Please write your honest reviews and experience of reading dark side of startup. You can also get a chance to meet personally with famous youtuber Mr. Arvind Arora (A2 Sir) and could also get a chance to win a signed copy from him.

**You can also share your views on the email id : thedarksideofstartups@gmail.com**

# Leaving an old job and working at a Startup for a higher salary

# 23

Up until now, everything we discussed was related to the startup, the startup founders, or the investors. Now we are about to shed light on a dark side concerning employees working in a startup. For an employee, their survival is most crucial. Everyone desires to work in startups, and this could be due to two reasons - first, learning, and second, a higher salary.

We've observed many people switching from well-established companies to startups. It's like they're saying, 'Let's create a storm today.' For them, it might feel like that. We believe that for a regular employee, this could also be quite risky. However, for you, it could also be life-changing.

We are about to narrate a story just like that, which is the story of an employee who switched from his well-established job to join a new and promising startup.

This is the story of Ankit, a talented young man from a middle-class family, approximately 27 years old. Ankit's job was at an IT company, where his annual salary was 18,00,000 INR. He was supporting his family very well. For a middle-class family, having a son with a good job was a significant achievement, ensuring them a decent life.

One of Ankit's friends who was working at a startup informed him that their company had received substantial funding from investors and was hiring skilled employees with attractive packages. Any opportunity with a higher salary couldn't be easily turned down. So, Ankit decided to interview for a position at the startup. He was selected, and the startup offered him a salary of 25 lakhs, which was considerably higher considering his age and experience.

To fulfill his dreams, Ankit first bought a new house and took a home loan with an EMI of around 40-50 thousand per month. He also purchased a new car with an EMI of around 20 thousand. Ankit's lifestyle was transforming rapidly. With the improved salary, he also got engaged and, for an extravagant wedding, took another loan.

Everything seemed to be going well. However, the startup Ankit worked for was facing challenges. The investment funds were depleting, and the prospects of securing new funding were diminishing. The company's founders decided to lay off their highest-paid employee, including Ankit.

The sudden decision by the startup put all of Ankit's plans in jeopardy. Now, his topmost concern was his survival. So, he began searching for a new job immediately. He managed to find a job in a short time, but his savings were running out by then. The new job offered him a salary of 20,00,000 INR, which was much lower than his previous salary.

With this reduced income, it was not possible for him to manage the existing EMIs and family expenses. Consequently, Ankit had to sell his car. He had to revert back to his old lifestyle. The place he had started from was essentially the same, but the difference was that he now faced severe depression and anxiety. However, he slowly managed to overcome these issues.

For Ankit, this was a significant lesson - in JOB, one should carefully evaluate any major decision related with any company and never switch from the existing company where you got a perfect job security until you find the same security in the new company. Decisions related to jobs and life should be made after careful consideration, because these decisions are intertwined with the lives of our families. Our incorrect decisions can jeopardize not only our own survival but also the well-being of our entire family.

*"In order to protect your job from layoff, you need to think about your Return on Investment as an Employee."*

- J.T. O'DONNEL

# Working in a Startup without financial and legal knowledge

# 24

From starting a startup to bringing it to completion, having a strong understanding of financial and legal aspects is crucial. Even today, over 75% of startup founders lack a background in finance and law. They heavily rely on advisors for these matters. Founders must possess legal and financial knowledge before launching a startup. While founders are becoming more aware of legal and financial issues, there are still relatively few who proactively seek to understand them. In a startup, lacking knowledge of financial and legal matters can lead to future troubles. We believe that some lessons aren't learned from mistakes but rather from taking an interest. However, sometimes mistakes do occur, and that's when taking an interest becomes necessary.

Now the question arises: how can we learn

about financial and legal knowledge before starting a startup? Whenever you're embarking on a task, especially one where you believe financial and legal advice will be necessary, take the time to thoroughly understand and educate yourself about it before you start. Discuss the reasons and rules with your advisors. Ensure that you establish processes to avoid any mistakes within your company.

Around 50% of your startup's success depends on your financial and legal knowledge, and it's better to learn from preparation rather than learning from mistakes. You shouldn't be giving yourself the chance to make mistakes due to lack of knowledge. As the saying goes, "Precautions are better than cure”.

"An investment in Knowledge pays the best Interest"

**- Benjamin Franklin**

# Sharing your Startup secrets with an employee

# 25

The biggest principle of Chanakya's teachings is that you should never reveal your secrets to others, otherwise doing so will destroy you. This same principle applies to business as well. Currently, in startups, founders have a lot of trust in their employees, and founders consider all employees as part of their family, because a founder spends the most time among their employees. Often it is observed that you can't keep anything hidden from your most special employee, and they are aware of everything related to the company. Sometimes, when there are disagreements between founders and their key employees, the employee can expose all of the company's secrets in front of competitors or others, which can cause significant harm to the company. Such situations have been observed among startup founders as well, where a founder, after leaving the company, exposes all the company's secrets, which can result in losses for the company or even the company shutting down. This is highly condemnable and unethical behavior.

> Be careful who you share your weaknesses with. Some people can't wait for the opportunity to use them against you.

# Engaging in any Startup activity without a contract and signing any agreement without seeking legal consultation

# 26

After startup founders receive funding, they often try to scale the company quickly. Many decisions are made promptly to ensure that the company meets its targets ahead of time. In the rush, the company undertakes a lot of tasks, and due to this haste, important agreements might be overlooked, or founders might sign agreements without thoroughly reading them. Not entering into agreements or signing agreements without consulting a lawyer and showing the agreement to a legal expert before signing can lead to trouble in the future. Many small and large startups are grappling with this issue. Their haste has entangled them in legal disputes today. Agreements are legal documents that can protect you from future troubles and also potentially ruin your career. Always remember that whenever you're signing an agreement, read it yourself and have your legal counsel review it as well, so that in the face of any future difficulty, the agreement acts as your friend rather than something that harms you like an enemy.

Startup founders should keep in mind that taking a little time to read instead of hurrying to sign agreements in the rush to fulfill a deal quickly is crucial.

In addition, if a company is engaged in any type of contract, founders should not proceed with the work without a proper contract or Memorandum of Understanding (MOU). It's important to carefully read all the terms and conditions of any contract and, whenever possible, involve the company's legal counsel in drafting the contract.

In many instances within startups, it's observed that the party to whom the contract is awarded is simply asked to create the contract, and work starts without thoroughly reviewing the contract, often with signatures obtained without proper reading. Startup founders, or their legal departments, should be cautious if such mistakes are occurring.

# Encouraging wrong habits driven by greed in the lure of free schemes and making more money, by Startups

# 27

Today, in the country, there are many startups that initially attract people with free services or offers using investors' money. They turn their company's products or services into a habit by providing them for free or with free offers. While this might be termed as a marketing strategy, some startups are causing many young individuals to waste their careers and time in pursuit of this approach. In the country, gaming startups and fantasy league startups create anticipation among the youth to earn quick and substantial money, leading young people to waste their valuable time and careers in this pursuit.

Numerous instances have come to light where the youth have become addicted to such platforms and have strayed onto the wrong path by investing money in them. These startups often promote youth icons during their marketing campaigns, which easily captures the attention of the youth.

Well, this issue is quite sensitive, but everyone's opinion can differ, as it can be viewed as a business endeavor, which can be very profitable. However, if looked at from a personal perspective, it can also be a path for the youth to stray. There's a very good saying, "If the service is free, you're the product."

**By Fantasy gaming we lose both our time and career these - two things are the most precious to the youth.**

# Violating certain specific regulations in a Startup

## 28

In startups, it's often observed that while preparing the business model, certain shortcomings remain, leading to violations of specific regulations later on. Today, in the country, some regulations are extremely strict. Neglecting such strict rules in startups can put the company and its directors in trouble. These regulations particularly encompass rules related to money laundering, regulations from SEBI, regulations from RBI, and regulations related to any criminal activities.

Many startups in the country have faced ruin due to legal actions, and during such times, startup founders have to endure a considerable amount of mental stress as well.

Startup founders need to understand the legal structure related to startups. It's essential to be aware of all the regulations that apply to the company while preparing the startup's business model. Even though startup founders might know the regulations, they sometimes overlook them. Such negligence can sometimes have severe consequences. Many times, startup founders are found saying, "We'll see when the time comes." However, it's important to be proactive and well-informed about the legal aspects and regulatory framework while setting up a startup.

This mindset might be suitable for a small business owner, but it can never be the thinking of an entrepreneur. Startup founders need to seriously consider legal regulations in the early days of their business. A proper legal structure strengthens the startup's business and assists them in achieving long-term success.

**Good Governance is the backbone of a startup.**

# Toxic work culture for freelance workers in Startups

# 29

The word "startup" itself implies that everything here will happen at a rapid pace. Stopping here is discouraged, as startup founders aim to quickly scale their companies. Nowadays, the startup culture has evolved in such a way that startups are becoming unicorns within 6 months to 3 years. But while observing all this, other startup founders are working tirelessly with immense enthusiasm, expecting their employees to work with the same level of fervor. However, this is where the toxic work culture starts in startup companies.

In startups these days, there is a behavior towards employees that's eroding their self-confidence. Behind the growth of any company lies the hard work of each employee. Their self-confidence is crucial for the company's growth.

Nowadays, startup companies promise Flexible Time, Leaves, a conducive work environment, and support from team members when hiring any employee. However, a few months later, they might ask you to work overtime without providing overtime pay. This situation can be exhausting, especially for freshers.

We have spoken to individuals working in various startups who shared that when they initially started working in startups, they were expected to put in hours exceeding 11 hours a day, much like freshers. The startup founders had high expectations for them to work overtime, yet they weren't compensated with overtime pay. They didn't receive any breaks (which they had earned), encouragement, flexible time, or anything of that sort. In this way, startup companies often target new employees who lack knowledge about work culture and ethics. This puts them in challenging situations, primarily leading to a lack of self-confidence, as despite putting in so much effort, their contributions are often overlooked.

Due to these reasons, the employee turnover in startup companies has significantly increased in the present times. Companies are often required to keep assigning new tasks to new employees, and within a few months, employees leave the startup's toxic work culture behind. This situation is quite unfortunate. If startup founders are addressing this issue, we would like to emphasize that making an effort to treat employees well is crucial. Treating employees with respect and providing a positive work environment is essential, as these are the very people who can contribute to the success of your startup.

> "A toxic workplace isn't only toxic for the people who work there, but also toxic for the startup's success"

## "THE DARKSIDE OF STARTUPS"

## YOUR THOUGHTS ON DARK SIDES OF STARTUPS

Name :

Contact Number :

CHAPTER REVIEW NOTE -7

Please write your honest reviews and experience of reading dark side of startup. You can also get a chance to meet personally with famous youtuber Mr. Arvind Arora (A2 Sir) and could also get a chance to win a signed copy from him.

**You can also share your views on the email id : thedarksideofstartups@gmail.com**

# Startup founders face challenges that can negatively impact their personal lives

## 30

The popularity of startups is on the rise across the world. Nearly 95% of startup founders are between the ages of 22 and 35. During this time, young individuals aspire to live their best lives. They want to balance work with spending time with their families. This phase is often considered the best, whether it involves traveling, relationships, or marriage.

However, you might be surprised to learn that the life of a startup founder can be very risky and exhausting. The journey to make a startup successful often requires them to work 15 to 18 hours a day without a break. Despite putting in such immense effort, it's not as easy as it might seem to achieve success.

It's true that even today, around 90 out of 100 startups fail. Now, you can understand the situation of those unsuccessful startup founders. The challenges faced by unsuccessful startups have a significant impact on their personal lives. The pressure of running a startup can affect their personal life as well. We've seen many founders whose personal lives have been disrupted due to their startup ventures. There have been instances where founders, after spending 5 years in a startup, didn't earn any money even after its closure.

Absolutely, the struggles of startup founders can deeply affect their personal lives as well. The saying "धोबी का कुत्ता, न घर का न घाट का" (The washerman's dog, belonging to neither home nor riverbank) often becomes relevant to their situation. Balancing personal life with the demands of a startup is incredibly challenging. At times, founders are faced with the difficult choice between their family and their startup. This is a heartbreaking situation for anyone. The harsh reality is that many startup founders end up sacrificing either their personal life or their startup aspirations.

The startup world can indeed take a toll on one's mental and emotional well-being. The stress and challenges can sometimes lead founders towards destructive habits and addictions. It's true that the journey of a startup founder can be very intense, and while it comes with its share of difficulties, it also provides valuable lessons along the way.

We have heard many real stories like this, where the pain of startup founders is evident from their words. One of our friends is also a founder who graduated from IIT Mumbai. He lost a lot during the time of his startup. When funding wasn't received, he took on debt funding, which he couldn't repay later. As a result, he had to give up his own home. His wife, frustrated, advised him to choose between the startup and the relationship. His family was greatly affected by his decision to start a startup. After about 6 years, the startup ended, and in return, he gained stress, family unrest, mental pressure, financial losses, and the wastage of time. Although after getting relief from the startup, founders do get their lives back on track, they can never bring back the time that has passed. This isn't the story of just one startup founder but the story of all those startup founders who have failed.

Failure in a startup is a significant matter, as even after establishing large-scale startups, many founders struggle to comprehend their exit strategy from the startup. It's quite similar to the stock market, where you remain profitable until you know the right time to sell your shares.

Amidst all this, there are also founders who use unethical means to make money during the funding phase of the startup. After this, several startup founders become influencers or investors themselves. We also urge you all not to make decisions solely based on the words of such founders and influencers, as you might have to bear the consequences. Make the decision to start a startup after careful consideration, and only then proceed with it.

*See things in the present, even if they are in the future."*

– Larry Ellison

# Starting a new after a failed Startup can be challenging for founders

## 31

We told you how startup founders face many challenges in their work life and personal life while starting a startup. Now, these challenges become even more pronounced after the failure of a startup. From here, making a fresh start isn't easy for startup founders. Opting for a job again instead of being an entrepreneur becomes a difficult decision for them. Additionally, they can't immediately think about starting a new startup or business, as they need to give themselves some time after the failure.

This period is painful for any founder, as despite putting in continuous efforts day and night, they feel like they're not making any progress. Moreover, the behavior of past startup investors, as well as the attitudes of employees, vendors, and others, can cause a lot of distress for them. Now you can understand that for startup founders, the first step is to break free from the past and then finding new opportunities is incredibly difficult.

However, over the time, founders usually manage to find their way, but embarking on a new beginning demands a lot of endurance and effort.

Due to the significantly high failure ratio of startups, you might come across situations like this around you. We have witnessed founders who are even older than 35 years struggling in such circumstances. We believe that when embarking on a startup, founders should always have a plan B in mind.

**The most dangerous poison is the feeling of achievement. The antidote is to every evening think what can be done better tomorrow.**

**– Ingvar Kamprad**

# Moving away of investors from their commitment to investment

## 32

Startup investment is currently a hot topic in the country. However, on the other side, delays in investment have become a significant issue. Recently, there has been a lot of discussion on social media regarding investment-related issues with Shark Tank India. Some startups seem a bit displeased with the delay in receiving funding after commitments made in Shark Tank. There have also been claims where startups haven't received funding even after investor commitments. Although investors usually conduct due diligence on the company before providing funding and might hold back if they find any discrepancies, some startups still face challenges in receiving funding after commitment.

Despite committing to investment, many startups often face difficulties when funding isn't granted promptly. This delay causes disruptions in the business commitments of numerous startups. Some startups urgently require funding, and the delay in funding puts them at the brink of closure.

This issue will always remain controversial because investors might perceive mistakes on the part of startups, while startups have their own unique set of challenges. If investors delay funding for startups after committing without valid reasons, it can impact the startup's operations. Similarly, startup founders should be mindful that during funding pitches, providing incorrect information to investors that leads to investment commitments isn't advisable, as the consequences of not receiving funding will affect their own startup.

In the world of startups, investment acts like oxygen, and sudden withdrawal of funding commitments from investors can potentially spell the end of a startup founder's career. It's important to recognize the delicate balance between startups and investors, as such actions can have far-reaching implications on the startup ecosystem.

# The Dominance of investors on Startup founders

# 33

These days, investors are often seen pressuring startup founders. It might surprise you that while founders are indeed the owners of their companies, they are also subject to revenue growth targets set by investors. When discussing larger corporations, achieving a Month over Month (MoM) growth of up to 10% is considered good. However, when it comes to startups, investors expect founders to achieve MoM growth of 20% or even higher. Due to these seemingly impossible targets, investors put a lot of pressure on startup founders. To appease investors, startup founders sometimes resort to unethical practices. Investors often expect startups to show fake sales figures and even bear the burden of GST on these inflated numbers. Many times, due to revenue growth targets, startup founders end up increasing their customer acquisition cost, leading to a significantly high burn rate for the company.

It's not far-fetched to believe that investors might have a role in pushing startup founders towards unethical practices to meet these targets. According to our assessment, investors, in their pursuit of quick returns, can inadvertently contribute to derailing a startup's organic growth.

Investors often put undue pressure on startup founders these days. It's essential to deeply contemplate whether startup founders are truly operating their companies as owners or if they have become puppets in the hands of investors. This revelation depends on understanding the situation of startup founders themselves. Investors exerting control over startup founders are not conducive to the genuine growth of startups. While investors contribute funds to startups, the time, career, and future of startup founders are heavily invested in the venture. When a startup fails, investors are not as adversely affected as the founders, employees, and vendors associated with the company. Sudden shutdowns of startups often lead to unemployment for many individuals. The responsibility for a startup's failure doesn't solely rest on the founders; often, investors are also accountable.

In reality, founders of even the largest

startups sometimes find themselves compelled to make unethical decisions under the pressure of investors. They are left to bear the consequences of these actions. The closure of a startup doesn't just affect its founders; it has a ripple effect on employees and vendors as well. The reality behind the glamorous facade of the startup world is that it involves much more pain and hardship.

On several occasions, you might come across instances on social media where startup founders are accused of fraudulently deceiving investors. Some influencers might portray how founders engage in fraudulent sales practices to deceive investors. However, the truth is that investors also push startup founders into situations where they feel they have no other choice. It's important to understand both sides of the coin in these scenarios.

> Think twice before you speak, because your words and influence will plant the seed of either success or failure in the mind of another.
>
> **– Napoleon Hill**

# Unit-2

# IMPORTANT INFORMATION RELATED TO STARTUPS

# What is necessary to make a Startup successful ?

# 34

To make a startup successful, it is essential to go through the following process:

### 1. Idea

As you know, the beginning of a startup is based on an idea. However, not every idea will be suitable for a startup. Behind a viable startup idea, a lot of work is required. This work is not as easy as it might seem. Nowadays, even friends can come up with startup ideas over a cup of tea at a tea stall, and there's nothing wrong with that. But creating a startup idea without careful consideration and then working on it is not the right approach.

An idea will only lead to a successful startup when it's solving a problem. In reality, searching for a problem-solving idea and validating it requires a lot of effort. It's possible that you perceive your idea as solving a problem, but there might not be an actual existing problem for customers in the market. Only a problem-solving idea won't work until customers actually need a solution. This means that your solution must be needed in the market for it to truly succeed.

It's not necessary for your idea to be unique. You can come up with an idea that modifies an existing business in the market according to your perspective. However, before copying any idea, it's crucial to gather information about the market's situation, competition, geographical conditions, margins, and market size. Many times, we've seen startup founders replicate ideas from businesses operating abroad to their own countries, only to end up unsuccessful. Behind this, factors like market conditions, customer preferences, and their needs, as well as geographical conditions, could play a role.

Before preparing and working on your startup, make sure to thoroughly validate your idea. This way, when you start working on executing an idea, you'll be better prepared to enter the market with a more robust business model.

**2. Planning & Execution**

Once you have thoroughly prepared your idea, the next step will lead you towards working on your idea. We've often heard that "Execution is the key to success." It's absolutely true that until you bring your idea into execution, you cannot progress towards success. If you need to transform your idea into a startup, you'll need to execute it correctly and work according to a well-laid plan. This is where the development of the product begins. At this stage, you'll require funding, which you can either obtain from yourself or from acquaintances. However, many times investors are also willing to invest as seed funding in your startup.

At this stage, you need to put a lot of effort into product development and testing because launching the product in the market comes after its validation. This stage is referred to as the pre-revenue stage. Here, if you secure funding, you often have to give more equity to the investor since the company's valuation is relatively low during this time. These types of investors are often known as "angel investors." They not only provide funding but also offer mentorship and expert support.

Startup founders in the product development stage usually obtain the MVP (Minimum Viable Product). After that, the product is taken to the market for sampling and testing. This way, you gather feedback from potential customers and understand the market. This helps in identifying the product's shortcomings before its official launch.

It's not as easy as it might seem while you're reading about it. Getting to this stage requires startup founders to work tirelessly day and night. If your product development isn't done right, you could find yourself out of the startup race early on. You come to know about this through product testing and market feedback. There are many startups that take a considerable amount of time at this stage, and by the time they're ready, market conditions have changed significantly. Therefore, in the development stage, you need to keep track of time as well, because product launching should happen at the right scheduled time.

### 3. Revenue Generation

When a startup completes its development stage, it means they have finished their product testing and sampling tasks. Now, the next stage for the startup is revenue generation. Generating revenue is crucial for any startup. Before launching their product, startups need to work extensively on marketing strategies, product costs, and the business model because apart from product quality, product costs can also impact the company's sales. Nowadays, choosing the right sales channels has also become vital for startups.

At this stage, the company requires funding again, as it needs funds not only for the team but also for marketing efforts. Startups can seek funding from angel investors, venture capital firms, or family offices.

From this point onward, a startup's ability to generate revenue becomes a determining factor for its success. You might be surprised to learn that nearly 70% or more of startups fail at this stage. The primary reason for this is that they either fail to secure funding or struggle to generate sufficient revenue.

Now, let's talk about what happens to startups that do secure funding. For those startups, there are two paths that they can take, and the choice depends on their strategies and decisions. One path involves focusing on revenue generation and, after securing funding, working on improving the product's margin to make it profitable.

The same alternative route, after taking the plunge, the complete focus of the company shifts to increasing sales. It is true that from here, the focus of a startup founder is on the product and its margins, more than increasing the company's sales, so that they can achieve a good valuation on the basis of revenue. In this way, their entire attention is solely on customer acquisition. Now, startup founders don't care about the profitability of the company or the product, because they know that in order to secure the next funding round, they need to make as many product sales as possible, whether or not they get margins on the product. Startups utilize the funds they have raised predominantly for customer acquisition. This is the stage from where the company transitions into the valuation vortex of growth and profitability, thus ending the hope of sustainable value over the long term. This mindset is called the Unicorn mindset. From here, only the valuation game and the story of hyper-growth begin. Hyper-growth means the company increases its sales numbers solely through customer acquisition based on sales and marketing efforts, and they don't care about product quality or customer feedback. The biggest risk of hyper-growth is the possibility of business failure. Anyway, nowadays, most founders in the startup culture operate according to the Unicorn mindset, and you are witnessing the results of it. Consider this as a prediction, but within the coming year, many unicorns will be on the brink of shutting down. The biggest reason for this is the recent failure of startup IPOs."

In today's scenario, startup founders are becoming better at pitching for funding, but unfortunately, they are not inclined to strive for becoming better at running the business. The experience of raising funds does not equate to the experience of running a business according to our understanding. Even while making their startups profitable and sustainable, you can still turn them into unicorns.

## 4. Funding Round

When it comes to startups, the discussion about funding happens right at the beginning. In different stages of a startup, funding is obtained at different levels. For instance, in the initial days of a company, angel investors provide seed funding. In the revenue stage, the company might receive super angel or some family office funding, which is crucial for the company's growth. As the company successfully begins its business journey and progresses with good revenue, Venture Capitalist (VC) firms show interest, considering the product-market fit and the business model. The journey towards becoming a unicorn starts here. During a startup's VC Series Rounds, there's a significant increase in valuation, as various options open up for them to advance in the market. On the other hand, startup funding is provided at different levels to propel the startup forward.

## 5.Exit Strategy

Someone rightly said that a startup founder doesn't become successful when they secure funding; rather, a startup founder becomes successful when they exit the startup at the right time and make money from it. It's important for startup founders to plan their Exit Strategy. A well-thought-out Exit Strategy benefits not only the founders but also provides investors with good returns. Generally, in startups, founders or investors have the following options for an exit:

- **Acquisition**: Selling the startup to a larger company that sees strategic value in the technology, product, or customer base of the startup.
- **IPO (Initial Public Offering)**: Taking the startup public by listing its shares on a stock exchange. This allows investors to sell their shares in the public market.
- **Merger**: Merging the startup with another company, often to achieve synergies or scale more effectively.
- **Management Buyout (MBO)**: Selling the startup to its own management team, allowing founders and key employees to take control.
- **Liquidation**: Closing down the business and selling off its assets, which can be a less favorable exit option.
- **Private Equity Buyout**: Selling the startup to a private equity firm, which often seeks to enhance its value and then sell it at a higher price.

Planning an effective Exit Strategy is crucial for both founders and investors to maximize their returns and ensure a successful outcome for the startup."

To build a successful startup, it's not enough to rely solely on a great idea; you need to put in hard work at every level. Whether it's about execution, revenue generation, funding, or the startup's exit strategy, you have to invest effort. Startups are a unique form of doing business, where you can certainly make profits, but even more so, you can earn substantial money in the long term by selling your business.

This is precisely why young people are drawn to starting startups. However, with the benefits of startups come potential drawbacks as well. When starting a startup, it's crucial to maintain strong business ethics. You should approach the idea of starting a startup with caution, considering all aspects thoroughly.

If you work with your conscience and carefully consider all the potential challenges and risks of a startup, you can lead your career to new heights. Startups indeed have the potential to take your career to remarkable places, but success demands meticulous planning, ethical considerations, and diligent execution at every step.

"THE DARKSIDE OF STARTUPS"

## YOUR THOUGHTS ON DARK SIDES OF STARTUPS

Name :

Contact Number :

CHAPTER REVIEW NOTE -8

Please write your honest reviews and experience of reading dark side of startup. You can also get a chance to meet personally with famous youtuber Mr. Arvind Arora (A2 Sir) and could also get a chance to win a signed copy from him.

**You can also share your views on the email id : thedarksideofstartups@gmail.com**

# What will be the legal format of a Startup ?

# 35

A startup is always aimed at rapidly scaling with great speed, and when a startup needs to scale quickly, it will also require funding. This is why the legal structure of a startup is often that of a private limited company. However, some founders in the initial stages of a startup might opt for a pilot project format such as Proprietorship, Partnership, or LLP, and later shift the startup to a private limited company.

A private limited company is a legal structure where startup founders raise funding from investors and, in return, issue them shares of the company. One of the most important features of a private limited company is that the management and ownership of the company are separate. The founders of the company manage the company's operations through the board of directors, while investors in the company do not have the authority to make day-to-day business decisions but, like the founders, are owners of the company.

In a private limited company, the founders oversee the business through the board of directors, while investors do not have the authority to make day-to-day business decisions, yet they hold ownership rights similar to the founders in the company.

### 1. Private Limited Company

In this, up to 200 members can be included through 2 shareholders. Most startup founders register a Private Limited Company for their startup, as it is appropriate if you need to raise money from investors in the future. However, there is more paperwork involved in running a company.

These days, growing startups find it easier to secure investor funding, and investors trust Private Limited Companies. The minimum authorized capital is 1 lakh rupees, but there is no limit to the minimum paid-up capital (subscribed capital). Selling the ownership of the company in the form of shares is easier in a company structure. Selling shares to investors becomes quite straightforward for startup founders in a company. Even today, more than 90% of startups in the country are registered as Private Limited Companies.

- **Limited Liability:** One of the most significant advantages of a private limited company is limited liability. The personal assets of the shareholders are separate from the company's liabilities. This means that the shareholders are only liable for the amount they have invested in the company and are not personally responsible for the company's debts.
- **Separate Legal Entity:** A private limited company is considered a separate legal entity distinct from its owners. It can own property, enter into contracts, and sue or be sued in its own name. This provides a level of credibility and professionalism that can be beneficial for business relationships.
- **Perpetual Existence:** The existence of a private limited company is not affected by the death, retirement, or insolvency of any of its shareholders. The company continues to exist, ensuring continuity of operations.
- **Ease of Ownership Transfer:** Ownership in a private limited company can be easily transferred by selling or transferring shares. This makes it simpler for founders to bring in new investors or exit the business if needed.
- **Fundraising:** Private limited companies are often preferred by investors for funding due

to the structured ownership and governance. It's easier to attract investment from angel investors, venture capitalists, and other funding sources.

- **Credibility and Trust**: Registering as a private limited company lends a level of credibility and trustworthiness to your business. It's seen as a formal and reliable business structure, which can be appealing to customers, clients, and partners.

- **Tax Benefits:** Private limited companies often enjoy tax benefits and exemptions that are not available to other forms of business entities. Additionally, companies can avail of deductions and benefits under various government schemes.

- **Professional Management**: The management structure of a private limited company, with its board of directors, provides a framework for professional management and decision-making, which can contribute to the company's growth.

- **Employee Benefits:** Companies can offer various employee benefits, such as stock options and ESOPs (Employee Stock Ownership Plans), which can be attractive for recruiting and retaining talented employees.

- **Enhanced Borrowing Capacity:** Private limited companies have better access to borrowing from financial institutions and banks due to their structured governance and liability limitations.

- **Brand Building:** A private limited company structure can help in brand building and establishing a recognizable corporate identity.

It's important to note that while private limited companies offer numerous benefits, they also involve compliance and regulatory obligations that need to be met. Consulting legal and financial experts is advisable when considering registering a private limited company.

**How to register a company in India**

To register a company in India, you need to follow a series of steps and complete various formalities. Here's a general overview of the process:

- **Choose a Business Structure:** Decide on the type of company you want to register. Common options include Private Limited Company, Public Limited Company, Limited Liability Partnership (LLP), etc.

- **Obtain Digital Signature Certificate (DSC):** At least one director of the company needs to obtain a Digital Signature Certificate from a government-approved agency. This is used for signing digital documents.

- **Obtain Director Identification Number (DIN)**: Each director of the company must apply for a DIN, which is issued by the Ministry of Corporate Affairs (MCA).

- **Name Reservation**: Choose a unique name for your company and apply for name reservation through the Spice Part A service on the MCA portal.

- **Drafting of Documents**: Prepare the necessary documents, including the Memorandum of Association (MOA) and Articles of Association (AOA). These documents outline the company's objectives, rules, and regulations.

- **Filing Incorporation Documents**: Once the name is approved, file the incorporation documents, including the MOA, AOA, and other required forms, through the SPICe (Simplified Proforma for Incorporating Company Electronically) form on the MCA portal.

- **Pay Fees**: Pay the required Stamp fees and other incorporation related fees based on the authorized capital of the company and other factors.

- **Certificate of Incorporation**: Once the MCA

processes your application and documents, you will receive a Certificate of Incorporation. This signifies the official registration of your company.

- **PAN and TAN Application:** Along with the Certificate of Incorporation the company will also get at the time incorporation of the company Permanent Account Number (PAN) and Tax Deduction and Collection Account Number (TAN).

- **Open Bank Account:** Use the Certificate of Incorporation and PAN to open a business bank account in the company's name.

- **Compliance and Registrations:** After registration, ensure compliance with various legal and regulatory requirements, such as obtaining Goods and Services Tax (GST) registration if applicable, and any other relevant licenses or permits.

**what are the important document required for the incorporation of the company**

The specific documents required for the incorporation of a company in India may vary based on the type of company and its structure. However, here are the commonly required documents for the incorporation process:

- **Director Identification Number (DIN):** Proof of identity and address (like Aadhaar card, passport, voter ID, etc.) of all proposed directors.

- **Digital Signature Certificate (DSC)**: DSC for at least one of the proposed directors. This is used to digitally sign the incorporation documents.
- **Memorandum of Association (MOA)**: A document that outlines the company's main objectives and the scope of its activities.
- **Articles of Association (AOA)**: A document that lays out the company's internal rules, regulations, and management structure.
- **Proof of Registered Office**: Documents showing the registered office address of the company, along with rent agreement (if rented) or ownership proof (if owned).
- **Identity and Address Proof**: Identity and address proof of all directors and shareholders, which could include passport, Aadhaar card, voter ID, or driver's license.
- **Passport-sized Photographs**: Photographs of all directors and shareholders.
- **Declaration of Consent**: Directors and subscribers must provide a declaration stating their willingness to become part of the company.

- **Form DIR-2 and DIR-8:** Form DIR-2 is a declaration by the first directors and Form DIR-8 is a declaration of non-disqualification by directors.

- **No Objection Certificate (NOC):** If the registered office is owned by someone else (not a director or subscriber), a NOC from the owner is required.

- **Utility Bill:** A recent utility bill (electricity, water, gas) as proof of address for the registered office.

- **PAN Card:** Copy of PAN card for all directors and shareholders.

- **Declaration of Commencement of Business (Form INC-20A):** This is required only for companies that have share capital, indicating that the company has started its business activities within 180 days of incorporation.

It's important to note that the documents required may vary depending on the type of company (Private Limited, Public Limited, LLP, etc.) and any changes in regulatory requirements. Additionally, some states in India might have specific requirements or additional documentation. Always refer to the latest guidelines and regulations from the Ministry of Corporate Affairs (MCA) for accurate and up-to-date information.

## 2. Sole Proprietorship:

If you want to start a company on your own, then this is the easiest way to start a company. Only a business registration license is required for this. It is especially popular among small business owners. You will need to open a current account with any bank in the name of the business.

- **Simplicity:** Setting up a sole proprietorship is relatively simple and requires less paperwork compared to other business structures.
- **Full Control:** As the sole owner, you have complete control over all business decisions and operations.
- **Direct Profits:** All profits generated by the business belong solely to you, as there are no partners or shareholders to share the profits with.
- **Flexible Decision-Making:** You can make decisions quickly without the need for extensive consultation or approval from others.
- **Tax Simplicity:** Tax reporting is often simpler for sole proprietorships, as the business income is typically reported on your personal income tax return.
- **Low Costs:** Operating costs are generally lower due to minimal legal and administrative requirements.

- **Privacy**: Sole proprietorships often provide greater privacy since there's no requirement to disclose financial information publicly.

**Drawbacks of a Sole Proprietorship:**

- **Unlimited Liability**: The owner is personally liable for all business debts and liabilities, which means personal assets could be at risk in case of business-related financial issues.
- **Limited Resources**: Raising capital can be challenging as you're solely reliant on personal savings or loans, making it harder to finance large-scale growth.
- **Limited Expertise**: As a sole owner, you might lack expertise in certain areas, which could limit the scope of your business.
- **Limited Growth Potential**: Sole proprietorships might struggle to scale due to the limitations on resources and manpower.
- **Dependency**: The business heavily relies on the owner's skills, availability, and health. If the owner is unavailable, it could disrupt operations.
- **Lack of Continuity**: The business might cease to exist upon the owner's retirement, death, or inability to run the business.
- **Perceived Credibility**: Some clients or partners

might prefer dealing with more established business structures, such as corporations, for perceived credibility.

## 3. Partnership Firm:

When two or more individuals collectively invest capital and start a business together with a Partnership Deed, the entity formed is called a Partnership Firm.

**Benefits of a Partnership Firm:**

- **Coordination of Different Skills and Expertise:** A partnership combines the various skills and expertise of partners, allowing the business to leverage knowledge and skills in different areas.
- **Pooling of Resources and Capital**: Partners pooling their capital provides the business with financial resources, enabling sustained growth.
- **Distribution of Specific Responsibilities**: Partners can distribute specific responsibilities among themselves, giving individuals a chance to work in areas where they excel.
- **Mutual Support and Collaboration**: Partners are likely to offer support and collaboration, which can be valuable during challenging times.

- **Open Communication:** Partnerships often encourage open communication, leading to better decision-making.

**Drawbacks of a Partnership Firm:**

- **Lack of Communication Among Partners:** Communication breakdowns among partners can affect decision-making.
- **Lack of Impartiality:** Partners may hold each other responsible for losses caused by one partner's actions, potentially leading to partiality.
- **Limited Organizational Lifespan:** The departure or incapacity of a partner can impact the business's stability.
- **Privacy Concerns:** Sharing financial and business information among partners may compromise privacy.
- **Complexity in Decision-Making:** Agreeing on personal opinions, perspectives, and goals can sometimes be difficult, leading to decision-making complexities.
- **Personal Liability:** Partners are personally liable for the firm's debts and obligations, which could put personal assets at risk.
- **Profit Sharing:** Disagreements over profit distribution can arise among partners.

## 4. Limited Liability Partnership (LLP):

A Limited Liability Partnership (LLP) is a type of business structure that combines the features of a partnership and a corporation. It offers limited liability protection to its partners while allowing them to participate in the management and operation of the business.

**Benefits of a Limited Liability Partnership (LLP):**

- **Limited Liability:** One of the primary advantages of an LLP is that partners are not personally liable for the debts and obligations of the LLP. Their liability is limited to their contributions to the LLP.
- **Flexibility in Management:** Partners in an LLP can actively participate in the management of the business, which allows for a collaborative approach to decision-making.
- **Separate Legal Entity:** An LLP is a separate legal entity from its partners. This provides a degree of legal protection to the personal assets of partners.
- **Perpetual Succession:** The LLP continues to exist regardless of changes in partners. The death or departure of a partner doesn't dissolve the LLP.
- **Professional Expertise:** LLPs are often chosen

by professionals like lawyers, accountants, and consultants due to their flexibility and limited liability benefits.

- **Tax Efficiency**: LLPs often have more tax planning options compared to traditional partnerships, as the LLP itself is taxed rather than the individual partners.

**Drawbacks of a Limited Liability Partnership (LLP):**

- **Complex Formation**: The process of establishing an LLP can be more complex than setting up a sole proprietorship or partnership due to legal formalities.

- **Limited Investment**: LLPs may face challenges in raising external funds compared to corporations.

- **Lack of Public Trust**: LLPs might face skepticism from the public or potential partners, as the concept of LLPs is relatively new in some jurisdictions.

- **Regulations and Compliance**: LLPs must adhere to certain regulations and compliance requirements, which can involve administrative work.

- **Decision-Making Challenges**: Decisions within an LLP may still face conflicts and disagreements among partners, leading to challenges in consensus building.

- **Limited Transferability:** Transferring ownership in an LLP might involve legal complexities and require the consent of other partners.

Overall, an LLP can be a suitable choice for professionals and businesses looking for a balance between limited liability and active involvement in the management of the business.

**Process for Incorporation Of Limited Liability Partnership –**

The process for incorporating a Limited Liability Partnership (LLP) can vary depending on the jurisdiction you are in. Below is a general outline of the steps typically involved in the incorporation of an LLP:

- **Choose a Name:** Select a unique name for your LLP that complies with the naming rules and regulations of your jurisdiction. The name should not be similar to existing business names and should include the words "Limited Liability Partnership" or its abbreviation "LLP."

- **Registered Office:** Decide on the registered office address of the LLP. This is the official address where legal notices and correspondence will be sent.

- **Designated Partners:** Identify at least two designated partners who will be responsible for compliance and obligations of the LLP. At least one designated partner should be a resident of the jurisdiction where the LLP is being registered.

- **Obtain Digital Signature Certificates (DSC):** The designated partners need to obtain digital signature certificates. These are used for digitally signing the incorporation documents.

- **Obtain Director Identification Number (DIN):** If required by your jurisdiction, designated partners will need to obtain DINs. A DIN is a unique identification number for company directors.

- **Draft LLP Agreement:** Prepare the LLP agreement which outlines the rights, responsibilities, and obligations of the partners. This agreement needs to be signed by all partners.

- **File Incorporation Documents:** Submit the necessary incorporation documents to the relevant government authority or registrar. These documents typically include the LLP agreement, Form FILLIP (Application for incorporation), and other required forms.

- **Pay Fees:** Pay the prescribed fees for incorporation, as determined by the jurisdiction.

- **Obtain Certificate of Incorporation:** Once the registrar reviews the documents and approves the application, you will receive a Certificate of Incorporation. This certificate confirms the existence of your LLP.

- **PAN and TAN Application:** Along with the Certificate of Incorporation the LLP will also get at the time incorporation of the LLP, Permanent Account Number (PAN) and Tax Deduction and Collection Account Number (TAN).

- **Open Bank Account:** Open a bank account in the name of the LLP. The bank will likely require the Certificate of Incorporation and other relevant documents.

- **Compliance:** Ensure compliance with ongoing reporting, tax, and regulatory requirements as per the laws of your jurisdiction. This may include annual filings, tax returns, etc.

# Startup Business Model

# 36

A correct business model plays a crucial role in making any business or startup successful. A good startup idea is one that can make the startup sustainable in the long term. This business model can set the standard for its success. However, currently, when a startup becomes a unicorn, it is considered successful. The journey to becoming a unicorn is not so easy, because the path to becoming a unicorn can also be determined by a solid business model of your startup.

To create a solid business model, working with accurate data and information is essential. Along with the business model, you need to pay attention to financial modeling as well, so that you can make your startup sustainable and profitable in the long term. Developing a business model is a fantastic process that structures every aspect of the business before starting it. Here, you validate your idea and deeply study various aspects such as product/service, customers, revenue, sales channels, market share, competition, product viability, product acceptability, risk, and many others. Only by crafting the right business model can you lead your startup to the pinnacle of success.

Let's briefly discuss some popular startup business models:

### 1. Freemium Business Model

(Freemium = Free + Premium)

In the freemium model, users are granted permission to use the basic features of a software, game, or service for free, encouraging them to become familiar and engaged with the offering. After some time, users have the option to pay a fee to "upgrade" and gain access to additional or advanced features.

Examples - Gmail, Google Drive, iCloud

### 2. Subscription Business Model

The subscription business model involves offering products or services to customers on a recurring basis in exchange for a regular subscription fee. This model has gained significant popularity across various industries due to its potential for generating predictable and steady revenue streams.

Examples: Amazon Prime, Netflix and Shopify

3. **Marketplace business model**

The marketplace business model involves creating a platform where buyers and sellers can interact and conduct transactions. In this model, the marketplace operator facilitates these interactions and earns revenue through various means, such as commissions, listing fees, or subscription charges.

Examples - Flipkart, Snap Deal, Amazon

4. **Aggregator business model**

The aggregator business model involves creating a platform that gathers and displays information, products, or services from various sources and presents them to users in a unified and simplified manner. Aggregator platforms add value by streamlining access to diverse offerings, helping users make informed decisions.

Examples: Ola Taxi, Uber, Airbnb, Repido

5. **Pay-as-you-go business model**

The pay-as-you-go business model, also known as the usage-based or consumption-based model, involves customers paying for products or services based on their actual usage or consumption. This model offers flexibility to users, allowing them to pay only for what they use, rather than committing to fixed plans or contracts.

Example: Amazon Web Service (AWS)

6. **Fee-for-service (FFS) business model**

The fee-for-service (FFS) business model is a payment structure in which customers are charged a fee for each specific service or unit of service they receive. This model is commonly used in various industries, including healthcare, professional services, consulting, and more.

Examples: Razor pay, Stripe, Paypal

7. **EdTech business model**

The EdTech (Educational Technology) business model involves using technology to deliver educational content, tools, and services to students, educators, and learners. This model leverages digital platforms to enhance and transform the learning experience.

Examples: Byjus, Vedantu, Physics Wallah etc.

8. **Lock-in business mode**

The lock-in business model, also known as the customer lock-in or vendor lock-in model, aims to create a situation where customers become dependent on a particular product, service, or ecosystem, making it difficult for them to switch to alternatives. This strategy seeks to establish customer loyalty and reduce the likelihood of customers moving to competitors.

Examples: Apple, SAP.

**9. Open-source business mode:**

The open-source business model involves creating and distributing software, products, or services under an open-source license, allowing anyone to view, modify, and distribute the source code. This model encourages collaboration, transparency, and community-driven development. While the software itself is often freely accessible, businesses can generate revenue through various means related to the open-source project.

Example: Andriod, Java etc

**10. Data as a business mode**

The data as a business model involves collecting, analyzing, and monetizing data to generate revenue. In this model, businesses leverage data they gather from various sources, including customers, users, devices, and interactions, to provide insights, solutions, or services that offer value to other businesses, organizations, or individuals.

Example: Open AI Chat GPT model

**11. Freeterprise business model**

A freeterprise is a combination of free and enterprise where free professional accounts are driven into the funnel through the free product. As the opportunity is identified the company assigns the free account to a salesperson within the organization (inside sales or fields sales) to convert that into a B2B/enterprise account.

Examples: Zoho and Zoom

**12. Razor blade business model**

The razor blade business model, also known as the "razor and blades" model, involves selling a primary product at a low or even subsidized cost while generating consistent and recurring revenue from complementary or consumable products or services. The analogy is drawn from the idea that the initial product acts as the "razor" and the recurring purchases of related products act as the "blades.

Examples: HP Printer & Cartage, Gillet razor & blades

**13. Direct-to-consumer (D2C) business model**

The Direct-to-Consumer (D2C) business model involves selling products directly to customers without intermediaries, such as retailers, wholesalers, or distributors. In this model, businesses engage with customers directly through their own online platforms, websites, or storefronts, allowing for more control over the customer experience, branding, and data.

Examples: Boat, Lenskart, Mama Earth, Sugar Cosmetics

**14. Franchise business model**

this model includes a franchise (store owner) and franchisor (company) where the store owner uses the trademark, branding and business model.

Examples: McDonald, Fabindia, Pepperfry

**15. Ad-based business model:**

this business model is used by the biggies of social media and search engine, that make use of the search engine and interest data to curate ads.

Examples: Yahoo, Google, Instagram

**16. Octopus business model**

This is a diversification business strategy, where each segment of the business operates independently but is attached to the main body, just like the extension of an octopus.

Example: Oyo

**17. Peer-to-peer (P2P) Business Model:**

provides a platform where two people can directly interact for the sale and purchase of a commodity without any middleman or third party.

Example: OLX.

**18. Brokerage business model:**

Normally works on the commission model, where they charge a commission fee from one or both the parties in return of mediating an agreement.

Examples: Zerodha, Coinbase and ebay.

**19. Drop shipping Business model:**

this is an e-commerce retail model that allows one to sell the products without any physical inventory.

Example – Amazon

**20. Space as a Service Business Model:**

Space as a Service Business Model is based on the thought of a shared economy that helps people to find a place to live or work either on ownership or lease mode.

Examples: WeWork, Airbnb.

**21. Affiliate business model:**

Affiliate business model this is a revenue earning strategy where they push the manufacturers of other companies to increase the production and charge a commission fee on each sale.

Examples: Amazon, Ebay.

**22. The virtual goods business model**

The virtual goods business model this is specifically for intangible products where in-app purchases are required.

Examples: Candy Crush, PubG.

**23. Cloud Kitchen Business Model**

Cloud Kitchen Business Model is also known as Ghost Kitchens, Dark Kitchens, Black Box Kitchens. This is basically a restaurant that sells its food through delivery partners without any physical dine in experience.

Examples: Faasos, LiveAltlife

## "THE DARKSIDE OF STARTUPS"

## YOUR THOUGHTS ON DARK SIDES OF STARTUPS

Name :

Contact Number :

### CHAPTER REVIEW NOTE -9

Please write your honest reviews and experience of reading dark side of startup. You can also get a chance to meet personally with famous youtuber Mr. Arvind Arora (A2 Sir) and could also get a chance to win a signed copy from him.

**You can also share your views on the email id : thedarksideofstartups@gmail.com**

# Process of raising fund in Startup

# 37

Today, in the minds of every individual, there is a desire to start their own startup. Doing business is also an art. Some people have the ability to do business inherently, and most of these individuals have a strong business background. However, the wave of startups has given birth to some young entrepreneurs, perhaps not initially skilled in this art, but through hard work and failures, they have made themselves so capable that today they have become well-known entrepreneurs of the country. Today, business and startups are viewed differently, and in my opinion, that's accurate. Business and startups are distinct, although in recent years, the popularity of startups has grown significantly.

Let's understand the difference between a startup and a business - in a business, the focus of the entrepreneur is consistently on earning profits through continuous and stable business operations. Business works right from the beginning on concepts of stability, sustainability, and profitability. Business owners gradually scale their operations while observing their capabilities and infuse money into the business as personal funds or bank investments.

On the contrary, in startups, founders focus on quickly scaling their startup to become a larger company. For rapid scaling of startups, a team is required, whether it's for product or service development, marketing, or managing the company's operations. This is why startups require initial funding. Startups receive funding from investors, and in exchange for this funding, startup founders offer a certain percentage of ownership shares in the company to the investors.

Startups also require initial funding to get started. In the beginning, almost all startups operate with bootstrapped funding. Bootstrapped funding means starting the startup with your own funds or funds from family members. Sometimes, startup founders need a significant amount of money to start, and that's why many good ideas fail because they don't receive funding for the initial startup idea.

After bootstrapped funding in a startup, founders often need investor funding to take the company to a larger scale. At that point, startup founders need to determine when, from whom, and how much funding to raise for their company.

Startup founders approach angel investors to pitch their startup for investment funding. Angel investors are individuals who invest in startups during their early stages and take a percentage of ownership in the startup in return for their investment. Currently, shows like "Shark Tank" on national television have popularized investment in startups. We have seen discussions on the topic of investing in startups and observed that in many cases, angel investors have also changed their investment into a share of ownership, often ranging from a few percent, in startups.

However, in reality, any company must go through a certain process before taking investment. Any company can raise funds from investors by adhering to specific rules. Startup founders cannot raise investment funds without following these specific rules. The checks given on shows like "Shark Tank" are merely for theatrical purposes and to create awareness about startups and their related issues. In reality, company founders have to go through a specific process to obtain funds from investors.

Funding in startups can come from various sources such as Bootstrapping, Angel Investors, Venture Capitalists, and more. Additionally, there are several other ways to raise funds, such as Crowdfunding, Incubators and Accelerators, Peer-to-Peer Lending, and so on. Currently, there are also government schemes available to provide funding for startups. This funding can be utilized for both starting a startup and scaling it.

Whenever startup founders approach an investor for funding, they should first and foremost have a well-prepared and accurate Pitch Deck. They should ensure that the data presented in the Pitch Deck aligns with the financial data of their company. Otherwise, your investment pitch might end up being just a sales pitch when investors ask for your company's financial data. This situation is common among many startup founders, especially when they manipulate data in their pitch deck or during their pitching to try to attract the investor's attention.

After founders pitch to investors for investment, they engage in deep-dive calls where they answer all questions and assure investors about their readiness to invest in the startup. Investors also discuss the company's valuation with the founders. Often, investors might reduce the company's valuation, and with the founders' agreement, funding is provided at a reasonable valuation. Once investor approval is received, a Term Sheet is signed. This marks the start of the startup's investment journey.

Before investing in the company, investors conduct due diligence, often through a professional Chartered Accountant firm, to identify any risks or issues before the investment. Sometimes, investors perform due diligence to understand the startup founders' intent. It's been observed that sometimes, due to an adverse due diligence report, significant funding rounds for startups can stall, putting a damper on founders' efforts.

For investment, the company issues shares to investors. Typically, companies allocate equity shares or Compulsory Convertible Preference Shares (CCPS). During the shares allotment process, company founders establish a Shareholders' Agreement (SHA) with the investors. This agreement safeguards the interests of shareholders in the future.

Here, we'll attempt to explain how a startup company (which is usually a private limited company) needs to allocate shares to investors while considering the Companies Act, 2013:

In a startup company, there are two different processes for shares allotment, known as Right Issue and Private Placement. Now, let's understand both processes:

**Right Issue:**

Right Issue is a process through which a company offers its existing shareholders the opportunity to buy additional shares at a discounted price. This is usually done in proportion to their current shareholdings. The purpose of a Right Issue is to raise additional capital for the company from its existing shareholders. It allows them to maintain their ownership percentage in the company.

**Private Placement:**

Private Placement is a method of raising capital by offering shares to a select group of investors, often institutional investors, private equity firms, or high net-worth individuals, rather than making a public offering. This method is usually chosen when the company wants to raise funds without going through the complexities of a public offering and wants to maintain a degree of control over who becomes a shareholder.

Both Right Issue and Private Placement are ways for a startup company to secure funding and raise capital. The key difference lies in the target audience and the process involved. Right Issue targets existing shareholders and involves a proportionate distribution of shares, while Private Placement targets specific investors and involves a more controlled offering to a select group.

In a Right Issue, a startup company generally offers its existing shareholders the opportunity to invest more funds and acquire additional shares. When startup founders want to raise additional capital from their existing investors, they adopt the Right Issue process. This method allows the founders to gather the necessary investment funding from the current shareholders. The Right Issue process is relatively straightforward and comes with simpler regulations and rules, making it a convenient option for startups looking to secure additional funds.

**The rules of share allotment under Right issue:**

1. A notice is circulated for the boards of directors meeting.

2. After the board of meeting approves the share allotment under right issues, the existing investors are offered to purchase the right shares.

3. If none of the existing investors are willing to buy the shares, the company can sell those shares to someone else as well, but they will have to get a right signed by the current investors.

4. After this, the company issues an offer letter to the current investors and other people who have agreed to invest. The offer letter has the

complete information about the investments and share allotment. It also mentions a specified period by when the investment funding must be transferred to the company's bank account.

5. This offer letter has all the information related to share allotment; it is submitted with the registrar of companies. It has a mention of all aspects related to the shares, like, what is the value of one share? How many shares are being allotted? How much money will the investor be transferring? How many investors have provided funds and how many shares are being allotted to them.

6. Investors transfer the funding amount to the company's bank account.

7. Now the company closes the offer letter on the pre decided date.

8. The registrar of the companies file PAS-3 form after the completion of the share allotment process.

9. one has to take care of certain rules under the process of Right issue:

- any pending open offer letter shall be closed.
- no offer should be advertised on ads, broadcasted or propagated on any public

domain

- Share allotment on the money received by the company should be completed within the next 30 days.
- the company has to mandatorily provide a share certificate to anybody who has received share allotment.

**Private placement:** is used to raise investment from investors other than the existing shareholders. This is a cumbersome process that involves a lot of rules which are needed to be followed by the founders of the company.

**Share allotment rules under Private placement:**

1. A notice is circulated for the boards of directors meeting.
2. After the board of meeting approves the share allotment under private placement, a shareholders meeting is organized following the approval of current shareholders.
3. The shareholders meeting is set up to take permission on the allotment of the shares to continue the private placement process ahead.
4. The company has to bring about a special resolution among the shareholders and the same proposal has to be registered by form

MGT-14 on the registrar of companies. The consultants complete this process on behalf of the company.

5. In this proposal, the company files the share allotment related information to the registrar of companies. It has a mention of all aspects related to the shares, like, what is the value of one share? How many shares are being allotted? How much money will the investor be transferring? How many investors have provided funds and how many shares are being allotted to them? On what valuation is the company allotting shares? And additional information related to the valuation and registered value.

6. After this, the company issues an offer letter to the potential investors who have agreed to invest. The offer letter has the complete information about the investments and share allotment. It also mentions a specified period by when the investment funding must be transferred to the company's separate bank account.

7. Investors transfer the funding amount to the company's bank account.

8. Now the company closes the offer letter on the pre decided date.

9. The company files a PAS-3 with the registrar of companies after the completion of the share allotment process.

10. Points to be taken care of under Private placement:

- Only a few selected people will get shares allotted.
- any pending open offer letter shall be closed.
- The given offer shouldn't exceed 50 people at a time , and 200 people in a year.
- The offer (a copy of PAS-4 form) should be provided to the identified people in advance.
- The amount received in return for offering the shares should be received only in a separate bank account.
- No offer should be advertised on ads, broadcasted or propagated on any public domain
- Share allotment on the money received by the company should be completed within the next 15 days.
- The company has to mandatorily provide a share certificate to anybody who has received share allotment.
- It is important for the company to maintain full information about the offer ( a copy of the PAS-5 form).

Now we will understand the technical terminology used in startups:

When a startup raises funding from investors, it occurs based on the valuation of the startup company. This valuation is essentially determined according to a valuation report. Before a startup raises funds, it's necessary to create a valuation report for the startup. Under the Companies Act, this report needs to be obtained from a registered valuer, while for income tax purposes, a valuation report needs to be obtained from a merchant banker.

When a startup allocates shares based on its valuation, both types of valuation reports are required for the allotment process. However, if a startup is a registered startup under the Department for Promotion of Industry and Internal Trade (DIPP), then there's no need to obtain a merchant banker's report for the shares allotment process. Instead, the entire process can be completed using only the report from the registered valuer. The cost of obtaining a merchant banker's report is generally higher, so smaller startups often opt for DIPP registration to save time and expenses.

**Please note the following points:**

- **Valuation Report:** The valuation report

accurately assesses the value of the startup, forming the basis of agreements with investors.

- **DIPP Registration:** Startups registered with DIPP are exempt from obtaining a merchant banker's report, streamlining their financial processes.

- **Valuation Professionals:** Choosing a registered valuer or merchant banker is crucial for proper and legally compliant financial processes.

- **Informed Decisions:** Making informed financial decisions is vital for startups to ensure accurate valuation and successful fundraising.

- **Equity:** The meaning of "Equity" is ownership in a company. Your ownership in any company's valuation will be your Equity. Similarly, if you're a sole proprietor of an entire business, then your Equity, which is your ownership, will be 100 percent.

### "Startup India" scheme

To benefit from the "Startup India" scheme, the first step is to register with the Department for Promotion of Industry and Internal Trade (DPIIT) of the Government of India. DPIIT, this department is responsible for promoting industry and internal trade in the country.

Startups that have DPIIT registration receive

a continuous three-year exemption from Income Tax. Additionally, those who wish to invest in your business also gain significant advantages. Therefore, if you have DPIIT registration, potential investors can show interest in investing in your business through the portal.

If, for any reason, you need to close down your startup, the process to do so is also relatively straightforward.

**Venture capitalists (VCs):**

also known by this name, are firms and corporations that gather funds from different partners (High Net Worth Individuals or HNIs) and invest that capital into various startups. Venture capitalists can appear similar to angel investors, but they are not the same. They are capable of investing a significant amount of money into a startup, making them more capable than angel investors.

Venture capitalists typically prefer to invest in slightly more mature companies, where they can see a positive cash flow and better revenue. This is because they view these companies as a better source of funding for growth-stage startups. VC firms' main objective is to invest in companies that have the potential for significant expansion and growth, which is why they tend to focus on companies with a track record of positive cash flow and revenue.

**An accelerator** is a short-term program that provides mentorship, network, and resources to small startups to assist them in their growth. Accelerators often exchange their services for either a fee or equity in the new company they are supporting.

**Debt Funding / RBF (Revenue Based Funding):**

This is a small duration loan ( 2 weeks to 3 years ), lent by investors to startup founders. If a startup needs funds to function while the investors equity funding is in process, the option of debt funding or revenue based debt funding is chosen to meet the requirements.

**Burn rate / Run rate**

Cash burn rate depicts how fast a company utilizes its funds in a given period of time. The startups with higher burn rate are always at a threat of utilizing the whole capital before becoming a profitable company.

**Exit Strategy :**

Startups founders ultimately have to transfer the ownership, so that they can earn profit for themselves as well as for the investors. A founder has many options to make an exit. He can make a merger with another company, sell the company or even get acquired by another startup or corporation.

**Growth hacking:**

Growth hacking is a marketing strategy that helps a business to grow faster at low expense by following non traditional tactics. The best strategy for growth hacking is video marketing, that makes short but interesting advertisements that easily get viral and promote the business.

**Pitch deck :**

A small, informative, attractive presentation that is used to explain the basic aspects of a company. It is shared with the investors to assure them about the morality of the company. A startup shouldn't miss out on mentioning the description of Product / services, business strategy and target audience while preparing a pitch deck.

**Pre-money and Post-money valuation**

Valuation of a startup before accepting any investment

Let's say, Two entrepreneurs, Ankur and Vipin are running their own high tech startups. An investor 'x' is ready to invest in their business. Both the parties, founder and investor, are ready for the investment. They are ready to invest 25,00,000 at the valuation of 1 crore. For Ankur 's startup, the investor 'X' is investing 25 lakhs at pre pre-money valuation of 1 crore. And for

Vipin, the same investor funds the same amount on post money valuation of 1 crore.

In view of this, investor 'x' and Ankur mutually agreed upon the proposed investment. 25 lakhs, on 1 crore post money valuation. On the other hand, Vipin's startup was valued at 1 crore before the investment of 25 lakh rupees. Now the value of his company is 1.25 Crore.

Equity owned by Investor 'X' in Ankur's startup:

Amount invested ÷ (Agreed Pre-money Valuation + Invested amount)

Equity % for 'X' = 25,00,000 ÷ ( 1,00,00,000 + 25,00,000) = 20%

Equity owned by Investor 'X' in Vipin's startup:

Amount invested ÷ (Pre-money Value + Invested amount)

Equity% for 'X' = 25,00,000 ÷ (75,00,000 + 25,00,000) = 25%

**ROI (return on investment):**

This is a performance measure that depicts how much profit an investment has made. A good startup should assure a positive return on investment and this calculation should be made prior to asking the investors for funding.

**Term sheet:**

Term sheet is a non binding document that specifies the possible funding terms and conditions. Normally, An investor signs a binding agreement for investment after approving the voting rights and ownership/equity percent share. This binding agreement is called a shareholder agreement (SHA).

## In the field of compliance, which specific things should be kept in mind, which need to be adhered to?

# 38

Running any company or startup requires paying attention to certain important compliances. Many times, startup founders face difficulties due to non-compliance within their companies. The founders of startups often come from engineering backgrounds and might lack knowledge about company-related compliances.

Let's understand which non-compliances can occur in a startup that founders need to be aware of - until the share allotment form (PAS-3) is filed, the application money for shares should not be utilized.

A minor non-compliance can lead to serious consequences for a company, as illustrated by an important case study. In this case, a private company submitted the PAS-3 return to the Registrar of Companies without filing the allotment return. The company utilized funds received from a private placement without filing the necessary documents. As a result, the Registrar of Companies imposed a penalty of ₹1,11,000/- on each individual involved in the company, including its officers, for violation of Section 42 of the Companies Act. This penalty was imposed to conclude the matter, and it was mainly due to the delayed submission of the e-form.

Due to time constraints, startup founders sometimes delegate tasks to their advisors or employees. In companies, founders often need to sign various documents at different intervals. However, due to the lack of time, they may not sign these documents themselves, and their advisors or employees may cut and paste their signatures from elsewhere. Afterward, these documents are submitted to the ROC portal.

In recent times, even such digitally manipulated signatures have been objected to by the ROC, and penalties are being imposed. Detailed information about such cases can also be found by searching on Google. For instance, you can refer to the case law of M/s Gozing Technology Private Limited, identified by the Case Law Number ROC/D/Adj Order/42/

Gazing/6967-6971.

This case study highlights the significance of timely compliance, especially in the context of technology-based startups today.

**If the shares are allotted under private placement without opening a separate bank account-**

When a company undertakes a private placement process, it is mandatory for them to open a Separate Share Application Money Bank Account to receive the Share Application Money. One should take care of the fact that the investment amount received during private placement can only be received in a separate bank account. A lot of times startups hurry to receive and utilize the investment amount and often ignore the conditions set.

A company did not open a separate bank account while receiving an investment under private placement. The company had to pay a penalty of 2,00,000 INR. "In the matter of Alpur Solar Private Limited Case law number ROC-DELHI/ALPUR/42/3709-3711 and A-42011/112/2014-ad.II"

## Pasting signature on a document:

Founders often are dependent on their workforce for daily and routine tasks.

Due to lack of time and hectic schedules, founders leave some of the tasks to their consultants or employees. The founders have to sign many documents on a regular basis. Due to their unavailability at times, the consultants or employees cut and paste their signatures, and later upload the same document on the ROC portal. Due to this issue, the ROC has started raising objections on the submission of such documents and discourages such activities by charging a penalty.

## Not mentioning the important information in the letterhead:

The letterhead should mandatorily have the name of the company, identification number, contact details like mobile number and email address. If a company doesn't mention the CIN in the official letterhead, they are subjected to a penalty of 14500/- INR imposed by ROC. "In case Law of GOAUDITS PRIVATE LIMITED F.No. ROCB/ Adj.454/Co.No.052650 /Section 12(3)©/2022/3018"

## Not taking care of the compliance of SFT while filing form 61A:

When founders accept investment funding, it is mandatory for them to file a SFT for the current financial year.

Company files SFT for investors who invest an amount of 10 Lakh or more in the company. This filing has to be submitted on the official portal of the income tax department. A lot of startup founders are unaware of this compliance and often ignore it during due diligence.

**Not increasing the authorized capital of the company before getting an offer:**

When founders establish a startup, they make use of funds equivalent to paid up capital. A company's paid capital can never exceed the authorized capital. That's why, whenever there is an increase in the paid capital, the authorized capital has to be increased prior to that. When a company prepares to allot shares to new investors, this means that the company has to increase the paid capital as well. A lot of times, the consultants even complete the process of share allotment, only to realize that the authorized capital has not been increased. This can put the company in trouble and further delay the allotment of shares.

**Not regularizing the additional director:**

An additional director can be appointed through two methods. Firstly, they can be selected by the board during a board meeting, serving as an additional director for a limited period. Alternatively, they can also be appointed through a shareholders' meeting. However, the appointment as an additional director is temporary. Once their designated term concludes, a shareholders' meeting must be convened to formalize their position, enabling them to continue their directorship.

In certain cases, startup boards might hastily appoint an additional director but overlook the essential step of confirming their appointment in a subsequent shareholders' meeting when the initial tenure concludes. Consequently, this lapse results in the director's term ending after the specified period.

**Allotting shares to a third party without renouncing it, under a Right issue :**

A company should know that the shares can only be allotted to the existing shareholders under a right issue process. If a company wants to allot shares to a third party, then they will have to get a renounce approved from the existing shareholders in their favor. This is a well documented process, which should be completed by the founders with the help of their consultants , without causing any delay.

**Error in the name and distinctive numbers mentioned In the share certificate and register of members:**

A company at times, mentions the wrong name or distinctive number while allotting the shares. This is a non compliance that shall be catered to while making the official documents. With the wrong name of shareholders, the chances of having a controversy increases. It might be possible that two people would fight with the company for the same share which would cost the company a lot of time and money. This particular instance has been seen quite a few times, you can refer to the internet to know more about it. "In the Case law of Vintage Hotels (P) Ltd. &Anr vs Ahamed Nizar MoideenKunhi ... on 12 November, 2020."

**Incomplete details of the investors while filing the offer details at registrar of companies:**

Company's Act states, if a company is allotting shares under the purview of a private placement, they should have the entire information about the investor, like their PAN details, contact information, email id, complete address etc. It is compulsory to attach all the investors' details in PAS-3 form with two attachments ( PAS-4 & PAS-5).

## "THE DARKSIDE OF STARTUPS"

## YOUR THOUGHTS ON DARK SIDES OF STARTUPS

Name :

Contact Number :

CHAPTER REVIEW NOTE -10

Please write your honest reviews and experience of reading dark side of startup. You can also get a chance to meet personally with famous youtuber Mr. Arvind Arora (A2 Sir) and could also get a chance to win a signed copy from him.

**You can also share your views on the email id : thedarksideofstartups@gmail.com**

# Process of Due- Diligence in Startups

# 39

Many times in startup funding, investors do not invest even after committing. The biggest reason for this is the discovery of irregularities, discrepancies, or unresolved issues within the startup company, which can affect the business in the long term. Today, startup founders feel more pressure in closing the funding deal than ever before, as they need to undergo the Due Diligence process. Due Diligence is the final step in the startup funding process, after which investors provide funding to the startup company. During the Due Diligence process, a detailed examination is conducted on the legal, financial, and business activities of the startup company. In this process, the startup company's data and information are thoroughly examined to ensure accuracy. It is in this state of accurate data and information that investors move forward with startup funding.

**We are going to tell you some important aspect of due diligence process of startup:**

In a startup, Due Diligence is a very crucial step for investment. During the Due Diligence process, a detailed examination and analysis of all aspects related to the startup's financial, legal, and business operations, strategies, products, and market are conducted. The potential risks and opportunities of the startup are assessed.

1. It's crucial for startup founders to organize their company before the start of the Due Diligence process. To expedite the completion of Due Diligence, startup founders should keep all necessary documents, data, records, and information in a single folder so that the entire data is easily accessible during the Due Diligence process. However, for the Due Diligence process, investor-appointed agencies often provide the startup with a Data Checklist to ensure that all necessary information is readily available for the evaluation.

2. Startup founders should establish a secure virtual data room where they can store their company's confidential data. This is the same place from which they can provide the data for the Due Diligence process.

3. During the Due Diligence process, it's crucial to have investors and their agencies sign confidentiality agreements to ensure the security of sensitive information provided.

4. During the Due Diligence process, various aspects of the startup are subjected to scrutiny, including Financial, Legal, Operational, Market, Strategic, and Management Due Diligence.

5. The objective of Financial Due Diligence is to assess the startup's Financial Health, Performance, and Projections. Agencies appointed by investors meticulously analyze all financial details, records, and relevant documents of the startup.

6. During Financial Due Diligence, a thorough review is conducted, including auditing the startup's Financial Statements, particularly those covering at least the past three years. Revenue and other financial metrics are analyzed closely to gain a comprehensive understanding of the startup's financial performance and trajectory.

7. During Financial Due Diligence, a review of key financial metrics such as gross profit margins, customer acquisition cost, customer lifetime value, and burn rate is conducted.

8. Financial Due Diligence ensures that the startup is paying all tax liabilities on time and won't be burdened with any additional liabilities in the future.

9. During Legal Due Diligence, a comprehensive assessment of the startup's legal structure, contracts, intellectual property, compliance, and any ongoing or past legal disputes is conducted.

10. Legal Due Diligence verifies whether the startup is properly registered with relevant departments. The review also includes an assessment of the company's bylaws and shareholder agreements.

11. During Legal Due Diligence, agreements with customers, vendors, founders, and employees are examined. Any significant agreements that could impact the startup's operations or financial position are carefully reviewed.

12. Legal Due Diligence ensures whether the startup has safeguarded its intellectual property rights through patents, trademarks, or copyrights.

13. During Legal Due Diligence, ongoing or past legal disputes, litigations, or regulatory issues that could pose risks to the startup's

operations or valuation are investigated.

14. Legal Due Diligence verifies that the startup complies with all applicable laws, regulations, and industry standards.

15. Operational Due Diligence focuses on assessing the startup's operational capabilities, skills, and scalability.

16. During Operational Due Diligence, the startup's supply chain is analyzed to identify potential risks and dependencies.

17. Distributors, channels, and partnerships are evaluated during Operational Due Diligence to understand how the startup reaches its targeted market.

18. Technology infrastructure, cybersecurity measures, and data security policies are assessed during Operational Due Diligence to identify potential weaknesses.

19. Key Performance Indicators are reviewed to assess the startup's performance and operational efficiency.

20. Market Due Diligence involves a thorough analysis of the startup's target market, industry trends, and competitive landscape.

21. Strategic Due Diligence evaluates the

startup's business model, growth strategy, and potential synergies.

22. Management Due Diligence assesses the management team's ability to successfully execute the business plan.

23. During the Due Diligence process, site visits are conducted to meet the team, inspect the company's operations, and understand the company's culture and work environment.

In the due diligence process, it is necessary to prepare while keeping all the issues mentioned above in mind.After the completion of the due diligence process, a Due Diligence report is prepared, and the appointed agency provides the report to the investors. Following this, discussions are held with startup founders regarding the Investor Due Diligence Report. Subsequently, investors may proceed with funding the startup or may decline to fund it based on the state of a negative report. Startup founders should be prepared for the Due Diligence process right from the beginning of their startup journey. If they are aware from the start, they won't make any mistakes in the future that could negatively impact the investment in the startup's funding round.